MY SON, JONAH

A PRACTICAL COMMENTARY ON THE BOOKS OF JONAH AND NAHUM

by

Cyril J. Barber

and

Gary H. Strauss

Foreword by Dr. Howard G. Hendricks

WIPF & STOCK · Eugene, Oregon

Wipf and Stock Publishers
199 W 8th Ave, Suite 3
Eugene, OR 97401

My Son, Jonah
A Practical Commentary on the Books of Jonah and Nahum
By Barber, Cyril J. and Strauss, Gary H.
Copyright©2005 by Barber, Cyril J.
ISBN 13: 978-1-60899-850-0
Publication date 7/14/2010

FOR OUR GRANDCHILDREN . . .

STEPHEN, JR., JENNIFER, KATHERINE, JONATHAN, SCOTT, and JOANNE.

CONTENTS

1. HERITAGE, VALUES, AND A MESSAGE OF HOPE   1
2. A TICKET TO TARSHISH   15
3. CAN WE RUN AWAY FROM GOD?   33
4. THE MARITIME CONNECTION   49
5. THE DEPTHS OF DELIVERANCE   69
6. FROM INSIGHT TO ACTION   87
7. A PRICKLY PROFILE   107
8. A MATTER OF TIME   125
9. WHEN GOD SAYS ENOUGH   141
10. NO LAUGHING MATTER   157
11. PUTTING PEACE IN PERSPECTIVE   177
12. CRABGRASS ON THE LAWN OF LIFE   195
13. MATURITY, INTER-DEPENDENCE AND HOPE   213

FOREWORD

Parenting is a bit like taking command of a full-masted schooner on an oceanic voyage, when our experience has been limited to the lake in our own little dinghy. It is the most important human responsibility and the one for which we are the least prepared. It is the only profession left to the amateur, and we need the expert help of the Master Teacher.

My Son, Jonah...and My People, Nineveh,, is a text for inquiring parents-at-sea. Most manuals on rearing the next generation are written with small children in focus. Rare is sound advice for older offspring beyond the author's experience. Cyril Barber and Gary Strauss have brilliantly worked off the model of God the Father to produce a theologically precise and psychologically -valid guidebook. Not only does the prophet Jonah dramatically define corrective discipline, he teaches the world a unique lesson about God's grace, and sets the scenery for Christ's enigmatic command, "Love your enemies."

The timeless "fish story" further comes alive in this exquisite parable about the power struggle between God's servants and their Creator. We see ourselves in Jonah. We touch the realism of tough love. When a father or mother can pick up the pulse of the Heavenly Father's heartbeat, family life will weather the storms.

This distinctive two-man authorship brings years of ministry and fresh, knowledgeable commitment to a subject much talked about, but often short on solutions. The team effort has produced a book that is readable and workable. It is ideal for use by individuals or groups, and the discussion questions enrich the study of the biblical text. This book should be added to the "must have" bookshelf of every committed believer.

HOWARD G. HENDRICKS

INTRODUCTION

What comes to mind when you think of God *the Father*?

For some, it recalls childhood recollections of a harsh, authoritarian parent to whom your mother reported your misdeeds and from whom you received speedy punishment. It is unfortunate, but our concept of God is frequently derived from the negative example of our parents, and Scripture seems to support this view. The writer of the letter to the Hebrews wrote: "Furthermore, my son, don't be angry when the Lord [disciplines] you. Don't be discouraged when He has to show you where you are wrong.... Let the Lord train you, for he is doing what any loving father does for his children.... If God doesn't [discipline] you when you need it, as other fathers punish their sons, then it means that you aren't really God's son at all" (Hebrews 12:7-8. *Living Bible*).

For others, however, the thought of God *the Father* brings to their conscious awareness recollections of early associations with their father and the warmth and affection, acceptance and security they experienced. When such is the case, it is easy to relate to God as a Father. It is also much easier for them to relate positively to their own children.

All of this seems simple enough, and yet we as parents still have to admit that we are faced with a problem; for even when our earthly father set us a good example, it is easy for us to become either too severe or too permissive in the way we rear our own children. And that is why we have written this book. It is designed to help you sort your way through these extremes. *My Son, Jonah...and My People, Nineveh,* is a work about the Fatherhood of God. It is also a book about parenting. And it develops a model of parenting-- particularly the parenting of adolescents--based on God's dealings with Jonah and the Ninevites. As such *it is a book with a selective approach and a special application.*

Two dangers have faced us as we have worked on this book. These dangers are similar to those that faced ancient seamen who traversed the Straits of Messina (between the toe of Italy and the island of Sicily) and have become known to us in literature as Scylla and Charybdis. The one extreme has been to be so concerned about exegesis that little or no attention is paid to matters of the Spirit. The other has been to produce a pietistic work which is blithely unconcerned about interpretation and slights the demands of scholarship. As with the seafaring men of antiquity who plied their trade on the Mediterranean and early learned to navigate the treacherous waters of the Straits of Messina, so we have attempted to steer a middle course between these two extremes. We have endeavored to combine our theological and psychological skills with a precise interpretation of the text, and have also attempted to accurately relate the teaching of the Word of God to the needs of people today. It is our belief that what God chose to reveal to mankind through the writers of Holy Scripture is relevant. Our aim has been to apply the teaching of the Word in a pertinent and appropriate way.

It may be that the title of our book appears somewhat inconsistent with what people have come to expect of Bible study. For this reason, a brief explanation is in order. Most commentaries on Jonah and God's dealings with the Ninevites focus attention on the person of the prophet, the history of the Assyrians, and the bricks-and-mortar details of the city of Nineveh. This is quite in keeping with the laws of proper interpretation. Others emphasize the missionary motif found in the Book of Jonah and stress the awesomeness of divine retribution which overtook Assyria. This is valid application.

But is this all? Soon after the turn of the century, the renowned 20th century British expositor, Dr. G. Campbell Morgan, observed that *"The essential matters of the book are the transactions between Jehovah and Jonah."*[1] Dr. Morgan's usage of the term "Jehovah" (sometimes rendered *Yahweh* and printed in many English Bibles in capitals as LORD) is most significant. It has special reference to God's Covenant with His ancient people, Israel (cf. Jeremiah 11:4;

---

1. G. C. Morgan, *Living Messages of the Books of the Bible* (New York: Revell, 1911-12), II: 228.

24:7; 30:22; 32:38; Ezekiel 11:20; 14:11; 36:28; 37:23; Zechariah 8:8; etc.) *and implies a Father-son relationship* (2 Samuel 7:14; Isaiah 9:6; 63:16; 64:8; Jeremiah 34:19; 31:9; etc.).

Picking up on this theme, we have studied the information given us about Jonah and the Ninevites from the perspective of God *the Father*. From our research has come practical ideas as well as informative principles for the rearing of children. We believe that by following the divine example God sets as Father, our sons and daughters will grow to adulthood mature in themselves, with respect for authority and able to assert themselves in appropriate ways. We also believe that under such rearing, children will have a greater possibility of achieving their full potential.

We have designed this small treatise for use by individuals, couples or groups. Couples may wish to use it as a guide for their own interaction on matters of child-rearing. And questions have been provided at the end of each chapter to prompt discussion. These should not be regarded as an end in themselves, but only as a place where one may begin to tap into the limitless resources and practical truths found in the Bible.

Throughout the writing of this book, we have been conscious of the many areas in which we have failed as parents. These failures have been a source of deep regret to us, and yet, they have also been the source of invaluable lessons we now desire to impart to others. God has been gracious. Our sons and daughter have reached adulthood and we are now able to see the ways in which God used these experiences, both positive and negative, as a means of growth. For this we are thankful.

In closing, we wish to express our sincere thanks to Maurice Bickley, David Cahn and Jan Hussey for preparing the manuscript for publication and making many valuable suggestions for its improvement. Thanks is also due Dr. Howard G. Hendricks for taking time out of his busy schedule to read what we have written and write the Foreword. We feel sure that our readers will appreciate the fact that the manuscript passed the close scrutiny of a theologian and educator before being submitted to the present publisher.

It is out fervent prayer that God the Father will use this brief work to bring special blessing to those who read it. With confidence in His Word, we commit our work to Him, for He long ago promised that His Word would not return to Him void, but would succeed in the matter for which He sent it (Isaiah 55:11).

Chapter 1

HERITAGE, VALUES, AND...
A MESSAGE OF HOPE

A junior high school teacher took her art appreciation class to an exhibit in a local gallery. As she showed her students around, she talked in glowing terms of the ability of the artists. Warming to her theme, she exclaimed enthusiastically, "A truly great painter can turn a smiling face into a frowning one with a single stroke of his brush!" On hearing this, one of the boys who had little interest in the exhibit was overheard to remark: "That's nothing, so can my father."

We can readily picture the scene. The tragedy is that we frequently look upon God the Father in the same way. For many of us, it may be difficult to think of Him other than as a stern, authoritarian Parent whose primary purpose (as far as we are concerned) is to stop us from having fun. For others, however, God may appear to be requiring us to live a certain way, but not involving Himself with us in the learning process.

The Bible speaks to correct these impressions. In the book of Jonah we have a remarkable revelation of God's mercy, compassion and loving dealings with His children. Many of us have grown accustomed to thinking of the book of Jonah as a "missionary" book; and certainly Jonah was a "missionary," but this is not all. As Dr. G. Campbell Morgan pointed out, *"The essential matters of the book are the transactions between Jehovah and Jonah."*[1]

The Backdrop of History

Jonah, we are told, was born in a small, rural village that nestled among the Galilean hills not far from Nazareth. It has been identified as modern *El Meshed.* In the days when he lived there, it was called Gath-hepher and was situated in the territory of Zebulun (Joshua 19:13). Mt. Tabor was visible to the south and Cana (the scene of Christ's first miracle) was only one mile to the northeast.

Jewish tradition claims that Jonah was the son of the widow of Zarephath, whom Elijah raised to life. He has also been identified as the youth who attended Elijah in the wilderness and as the young man who anointed Jehu king over Israel. These traditions may be dismissed, for they lack verifiable evidence and place Jonah at a juncture of Israel's history which is considerably before the time of Jeroboam II (2 Kings 14: 23, 25).

Jonah was probably born in the Northern Kingdom of Israel during the reign of Jehoahaz (814-798 B.C.). Throughout his boyhood, the fortunes of the northern tribes of Israel were constantly changing (2 Kings 10:32-33). The

---

1. Morgan, *Living Messages of the Books of the Bible*, II: 228.

Syrians and the Assyrians repeatedly invaded the land, and those kings who exhibited some military prowess were often found to be poor administrators. Consequently, the fifty years that preceded Jonah's birth saw unrest and turmoil. As a result, serious social and economic problems had developed (2 Kings 13:7).

Some relief came to the Israelites when Jehoahaz made an alliance with the Assyrians (2 Kings 13:1-9). Adad-nirari III of Assyria,[2] (810-783 B.C.)[3] attacked Damascus and completely subdued the Syrians (803 B.C.). Now Israel, along with several other countries who had bought Assyrian help, had to pay heavy taxes to their new Assyrian "lords." This served to increase the oppression they already felt.

Jehoahaz' reign did not last very long, and on his death be was succeeded by his son, Jehoash (798-782 B.C.; 2 Kings 13:10-25; 14:15-16). Jehoash (or Joash as he was also called) strengthened the position of Israel and made

---

2. For documents pertaining to the reign of this Assyrian monarch, see *Ancient Near Eastern Texts* (2d ed.; Princeton: Princeton University Press, 1959), pp. 281-82; and D. W. Thomas, *Documents from Old Testament Times* (New York: Harper, 1958), pp. 50-52.
3. For the chronology of the period and the co-rulership of Joash and Jeroboam II, see E. R. Thiele's *Mysterious Numbers of the Hebrew Kings* (rev. ed.; Grand Rapids: Eerdmans, 1965), pp. 73ff.

rapid strides along the road to recovery. He was a very sensitive king and early in his administration sought the counsel of the aged prophet Elisha. The Syrians were again threatening Israel's autonomy, and Elisha predicted that under Jehoash's leadership Israel would defeat them.

After Jehoash had ruled for only five years, Amaziah, king of Judah, attacked the southern border of Israel. Jehoash placed his son, Jeroboam II (793-753 B.C.; 2 Kings 14:23-29)[4] on the throne before engaging Amaziah in battle (2 Kings 14:1-14). The battle was a decisive one, and Jehoash returned to Samaria laden with the spoils of war. It was soon after Jehoash's death, when Jeroboam II had taken over as supreme ruler of Israel, that Jonah predicted the military success of the new king. For this prophecy, he received considerable acclaim at court and became very popular with the people.

Man With a Future

But how did Jonah rise from obscurity to a position of influence and esteem? And what was there in the way he was reared that prepared him for such a ministry?

---

4. See W. F. Albright's Goldenson Lecture, "Samuel and the Beginnings of the Prophetic Movement in Israel," Hebrew Union College, 1961; and his book *Yahweh and the Gods of Canaan* (Garden City, NY: Doubleday, 1968), pp. 208-213.

Jonah's father was a man named Amittai. The name means "true, faithful," and from what we know of his son it would seem as if he lived up to his name. Amittai was evidently a worshiper of the true God and must have been one of the ever-decreasing group of God-fearing men who served the Lord in the midst of increasing secularism and spiritual decline. Such men are "the salt of the earth," and, while little is known of them and their names may never make the front page of the newspaper, their influence nevertheless is felt by those about them. The impact of Amittai's example must have left its mark on Jonah, for it provided him with a godly model to follow, contributed to a stable home environment, and gave Jonah a secure foundation on which to build his own life of devotion to the Lord.

The little village into which Jonah was born would also have left its impress on him. In rural communities, children often learn early in life the dignity of work and the importance of honesty. They typically have instilled in them a high idealism, and in this conservative environment the differences between black and white are clearly set forth. The result is often the development of reliability and the emergence of firm convictions, which last throughout their lifetime.

In the course of time the high idealism Jonah had inherited from his father and developed in the community in which he was reared was reinforced when he enrolled in "the School of the Prophets." This movement had its beginnings with Samuel and exerted an influence for good in

Israel. It is highly probable that Jonah had the privilege of sitting under the ministry of the elderly Elisha and learning from him the ways of the Lord.

Elisha is one of the colorful characters of the Old Testament. He appears on the pages of God's Word as a seemingly harsh and awesome figure; and yet, in contrast to Elijah, he lived among the people and was well liked by those who knew him. From what we read of Elisha, it appears as if he was the kind of person who did not settle for half measures. The times of spiritual apostasy through which Israel was passing called for total dedication to the Lord, and those who gathered about the aged prophet obviously shared his commitment.

It is not hard for us to imagine how contact with a person such as Elisha would fan Jonah's idealism. He became a man of convictions, and came to see more clearly than ever before how sin was robbing the nation of God's blessings. The times were too serious for him to be mediating; and with firm principles undergirding his beliefs, Jonah became a staunch patriot. He adhered unalterably to the theocracy[5] and believed that spiritual renewal would lead to national recovery.

---

5. Theocracy" comes from two Greek words, *theos*, "God, and *kratein*, "to rule." Its usage refers to "the rule of God through a divinely chosen representative who speaks and acts for God but also represents the people before God." See A. J. McClain, *The Greatness of the Kingdom* (Chicago: Moody, 1968), p. 41.

Later on, after graduating from Elisha's "seminary," Jonah began his ministry in Samaria. Here, as we have seen, he achieved fame when he predicted the success of a war Jeroboam was to wage against Syria. Inspired by this prophecy, Jeroboam recovered land formerly lost to their enemies, and extended the borders of Israel as far north as had Solomon (cf. 2 Kings 14:23-28 with 1 Kings 8:65). From this time onwards, Jonah's future was assured. He was for all intents and purposes "chaplain to the king."

Note of Defiance

Then the unexpected happened. God commissioned Jonah to go and preach to the people of Nineveh. But Jonah feared the conversion of these Gentiles. They were Israel's enemies. At this point his pride of race clouded his perspective and he may have reasoned, "If I preach to them they will repent and God will then use them to chasten Israel." He therefore chose to disobey God and fled instead to Tarshish (Jonah 1:1-2).

God, however, was not to be out-maneuvered. By means of a storm at sea, He showed Jonah His displeasure. The pagan sailors recognized His power and repented of their sins. Only Jonah remained obstinate. He preferred drowning to going to Nineveh and suggested that the sailors throw him overboard. With great reluctance, they did as he requested (Jonah 1:3-16).

Being far from land, Jonah knew that he could not survive in such heavy seas and was prepared to drown rather than be the means of bringing the Assyrians to repentance.

But God was not caught off guard by His recalcitrant son. He prepared a great fish to swallow Jonah. In the belly of the fish Jonah finally repented. When he did so, he was disgorged and recommissioned to go to Nineveh (Jonah 1:17-2:10).

While Jonah was now obedient, it was a reluctant kind of obedience, and when he reached Nineveh his preaching was not calculated to inspire confidence or lead the people to repentance. Why then did the people of Nineveh repent? The Lord Jesus tells us that Jonah was "a sign" to the people of Nineveh (Luke 11:30). From this statement we deduce that when the people of Nineveh saw the effects of God's judgment on him (for Jonah's body had been bleached by the gastric juices in the fish's body), they repented of their sins (Jonah 3).

But such repentance did not please the prophet of Israel, and God had to deal with him in much the same way that a father deals with a rebellious child (Jonah 4).

So far the movements of the story are easy to follow. Someone, however, is sure to ask, "But who wrote these memoirs?" To this question there can be one possible answer: Jonah. If this is so, then there is an unwritten "postscript" to the book. Jonah must have finally come to see things God's way and repented of his pride and disobedience. The book, however, is written in the third person, and this may indicate that someone else, perhaps a student in the School of the Prophets, recorded the story exactly as Jonah told it. On the other hand, for an author to write in the third person was a common phenomenon in Bible times. But if someone else wrote the book, then he served in a similar capacity to those students who gathered about Martin Luther, recorded his sayings, and bequeathed to posterity the great reformer's *Table Talk*.

Differing Interpretations

The book of Jonah has been criticized and ridiculed more than any other book in the Old Testament. Those who poke fun at it do so on account of its miraculous element. They are not prepared to accept the miraculous, and attempt to justify their rejection of it by claiming that the book is a parable with a didactic message of encouragement to a beleaguered people. Others claim that it is a "story" that propounds a moral principle. This makes the book as authentic as a fairy tale or one of the apocryphal or pseudepigraphal works that have no part in the canon of inspired Scripture.

Still other writers treat the contents as an allegory and spiritualize the text in their quest for principles that will be meaningful to Christians today. And some even find a prophetic element in the book. They claim that Jonah's experiences in the belly of a "great fish" foreshadow the future of the Jewish people during the Tribulation period.

In spite of these claims, Jonah's mission to Nineveh was obviously historical. Jewish rabbis and historians such as Josephus have regarded it in this way. And the Lord Jesus Himself referred to the prophet's experiences as foreshadowing His death (Matthew 12:38-42; 16:4; Luke 11: 29-32). Such an appeal would be ludicrous if the events in Jonah's life were not historical.

Of far greater value is the literal interpretation of the text that sees in the commission of Jonah the real experiences of a disobedient prophet. It also reveals God's love for the lost and contains His implied rebuke of the spiritual pride and insularity of the nation of Israel–a situation that parallels the condition of some segments of the Christian church today.

Inasmuch as other writers have dealt adequately with the theme of missions, our purpose will be to focus attention on God the Father and His dealings with His creatures: His willful prophet, the impressionable sailors, the people of Nineveh, and finally, the way in which He melted the stubbornness of his loyal but misguided servant. The objections of critics to the miraculous will also be dealt with, but in a way that will not detract from the purpose of this work.

As we study these chapters together, we will find that God has a great deal to teach us about our relationship with

Him. And Christian parents, by modeling themselves after the pattern set by God the Father, will be better equipped to relate to their teenage sons and daughters in the variety of circumstances they face.

Was Nineveh Ever Punished?

Whereas, in the book of Jonah, God is seen dealing with a rebellious child, in the divine "sequel" we see the Lord dealing with the people of Nineveh in terms of their waywardness. What, then, will be the practical benefit to us of this material? From a study of God's dealings with Jonah we learn how to direct the activities of our sons and daughters; what to do when they close the door to communication; the manner and the means of appropriate discipline; and how to build and maintain their sense of worth. And from God's dealings with the Assyrians we learn the importance of maturity and how we may guide those in our homes toward responsible adulthood.

The "sequel" to Jonah's experiences will also restore our perspective of reality. We will come to see more clearly than ever before God's sovereignty and our accountability before Him. And those who, beset by the trials and difficulties of parenting, ask, "Has God abandoned me? I try to do my best for my children, yet without success," or who question, "If God is sovereign, why does He permit the ungodly to prosper?" will find their faith strengthened by what is recorded of Assyria's later experiences.

INTERACTION

1. In 2 Kings 13:14-19 the aged prophet Elisha is dying. His body is in a weakened condition. The king visits him and unwittingly causes Elisha to become angry. Consider first Elisha's patriotism, and then discuss the kind of influence he would have exerted on a young man as impressionable as Jonah.

2. Jonah came from a small, rural community. What advantages are there to rearing one's sons and daughters in such an environment? What disadvantages?

3. True maturity is attained through the practice of three things: (a) A knowledge of the Word of God and the application of its teaching to everyday life (Hebrews 5:13-14); (b) Fellowship with God and His people (Hebrews 10:23-25); and (c) our personal witness (Hebrews 12:28). In what ways was Jonah prepared, by the training he received and the examples he had for (a) and (b)? Why was he unprepared for (c)?

4. In rearing our sons and daughters we try to instill in them a spirit of discernment--the ability to distinguish between right and wrong. Sometimes this results in their disliking people as well as their practices. This was Jonah's problem. He knew that God was "slow to anger and abundant in loving kindness" (Jonah 4:2), and yet disobeyed Him because he hated those in Nin-

eveh. "On the human plane I can understand him perfectly," said Dr. G. Campbell Morgan; "Nineveh was guilty of cruelty and abominations for which one hundred years later another prophet uttered her doom. She was merciless and cruel, and Jonah was in rebellion against her being spared." How did God lead Jonah to discover that anger with sin is born of love for the sinner? In what ways will this truth transform our witness?

5. Take a piece of paper and divide it down the middle. Give one column the heading GOD and the other the heading JONAH. Read through the book of Jonah and make a list of all the emotions ascribed to either God or Jonah (e.g., anger, fear, love [implied], despair, happiness, etc.). What do these teach us (a) about God, and (b) human nature?

NOTES

Chapter 2

A TICKET TO TARSHISH

One of the best known stories of the New Testament is the parable of the prodigal son (Luke 15:11-27). It sets forth in clear and unmistakable terms God's love for sinners. Not as well known is the story of "the other brother" (Luke 15:28-32). In his denunciation of his wayward brother, he reveals his own estimate of himself. He is conscious of his moral rectitude and sees himself as a model son. However, in emphasizing the fact that he has "served his father as a slave" (Luke 15:30), he shows that he does not really know what sonship means.

The parable of the prodigal son is, in reality, a parable of the heart of God. In much the same way that the father of these two boys went out to welcome home the erring youth, so now he goes out to plead with his self-righteous son. His words to his older son are tender and appealing. He loves both his children. He makes it clear that he appreciates his elder son's loyalty and service. Then, by emphasizing the words "your brother" (in contrast to the older boy's "your son," Luke 15:30), his father reminds him of his relationship.

In this parable we tend to see ourselves as "prodigals" coming to the welcoming love and warm embrace of God the Father. This is true of all sinners who turn to Him in repentance. But is it not also true that we may see ourselves as the elder brother? Following our conversion, isn't it possible for us to become so identified with our "religious, church-going set" that we have little true compassion towards those who are lost? Isn't possible that in our self-righteous pride we may become judgmental of those who do not live up to our standards?

In the scene before us (Jonah 1:1-3), Jonah finds himself in just such a position. As he relates his story, he tells us that "the word of Yahweh came to him saying, 'Arise, go to Nineveh the great city, and proclaim against it; for their wickedness has come up before Me [lit., before My face].'" His response, however, is one of hostile disobedience, and it is necessary for God to intervene. In doing so, He teaches Jonah (and us) the lesson of His fatherly concern for those who are lost.

A Question of Loyalties

The narrative begins with the word "and." It is translated in most versions as "now." This makes better reading; at least as far as our Western minds are concerned. To a Hebrew, however, beginning a book with the word "and" did not do violence to their literary sensitivity (see Exodus 1:1; Leviticus 1:1; Numbers 1:1; Joshua 1:1; Judges 1:1; Ruth 1:1; 1 Samuel 1:1; 2 Samuel 1:1; 1 Kings 1:1; 2 Kings 1:1; Esther 1:1; Ezra 1:1; Nehemiah 1:1b; 2 Chronicles 1:1), for it placed the writing in the mainstream of Bible history.

By beginning his story with the word "and," Jonah reminds us of the unity of God's Word, and connects his writings with the rest of God's inspired revelation.

When God speaks to Jonah, it is as to a responsible and intelligent participant with Him in His work. His instructions are clear and direct. "Arise," He says, "Go . . . proclaim." The usage of His name, *Yahweh* (LORD),[1] is designed to give "parental" reassurance to Jonah. It is as if God, recognizing Jonah's possible anxiety over his coming assignment, is saying to him: "You are My son. You have a special place in My heart. I want you to go on an important mission to Nineveh and bring them the message of My love."

In this connection we, as parents, need to be sensitive to the possible fears and apprehensions our children experience in situations they may be facing. Supportive communication on our part may give our children the unsolicited, but needed reassurance of the special place they have in our lives. God's attitude toward Jonah brings to mind a story we heard recently. A couple in the Midwest had one son by natural birth and then, unable to have any more children,

---

1. The Hebrew term *Yahweh* is used frequently in the Bible. It refers to God as the self-existent One, and is used of Him in relation to His people as their covenant-keeping God. The basic connotation of the term *Yahweh* is holiness. It is a particularly appropriate term in this book for it deals with God, His covenant relationship with His people, and the people of Assyria.

decided to adopt another. The two boys grew up together and one day, while playing in front of the house, were questioned by a stranger about their relationship. "Oh," replied the younger son, "one of us is adopted, but I forget which one." He had been given such reassurance that, although he was adopted, it was no longer a question of significance in terms of his security.

In the case of Jonah, Israel was the natural "son." To them belonged a special "sonship." They were the recipients of the covenants and the Law and the service of the Temple and the promises given to the Fathers (Romans 9:4-5); but they were unwilling to share these blessings with anyone else.[2] God, the Creator of all things, loved both Israel and the surrounding nations. This included Assyria. In commissioning Jonah to go to Nineveh, He was, in reality, reaching out to a "lost son."

Unfortunately, Jonah's reaction to the command of the Lord was similar to "the other brother" in Luke's parable. He was jealous of Israel's position as God's chosen people. Assyria had already shown its oppressive hand. Shalmaneser III had warred against Ahab and, later on, received taxes from Jehu; and Adad-nirari III had imposed tribute on Israel. Jonah knew that Israel's waywardness was inviting God's chastisement and that, while the political and military morale of the Assyrians was now at a low ebb, God would not judge Assyria if they turned to Him in penitence.

The Legacy of History

As a city, Nineveh had a long history. It had been founded by Nimrod (Genesis 10:11), whom the Bible describes as "a mighty one on the earth" (Genesis 10:8-9). His prowess became proverbial so that even Micah, writing in the eighth century B.C., refers to Assyria as the land of Nimrod (Micah 5:6). Nimrod first settled in Shinar (ancient Mesopotamia, see Genesis 10:10). From there he went to Assyria where he built Nineveh and three other cities.

The original city of Nineveh lay on the east side of the Tigris River, opposite the modern town of Mosul. Its ruins consist chiefly of two great mounds, Kouyunik and Nebi

---

2. The teaching of the Fatherhood of God has become one of the major tenets of theological liberalism, and is used to support its belief in universal salvation. Evangelicals, therefore, have reacted against this teaching, even to denying it altogether (cf. L. Strauss, *The First Person* [Neptune, NJ: Loizeaux, 1967], pp. 117-125). To properly understand what is involved, we need to keep distinct in our minds the Fatherhood of God over all creation (Isaiah 64:8c; Malachi 2:10; Acts 10:10-16, 28, 34-35; 17:24-26, 29; 1 Corinthians 8:6), and His special relationship to the redeemed. Salvation is *not* a part of the first (Romans 9:8); it is the basis of the second (Romans 8:15). Both experience the initiative of God's love quite apart from any merit in the object (Isaiah 64:6). Humans in their natural, unregenerate state are the enemy of God (Colossians 1:21). Only by repenting of one's sin and accepting Christ as Savior can a person become a child of God (Romans 5:8, 10). When this happens, God becomes one's Father in a redemptive sense (Galatians 3:26; 1 John 3:10).

Yunas, and the remains of the city walls. The fact that one of the mounds is called Nebi Yunas (Prophet Jonah) is evidence of the deep-seated belief that Jonah visited Nineveh. The river Khoser that rises in the mountains to the east flows between the two great mounds into the Tigris. Archaeologists have unearthed the palaces of Sennacherib and Ashurbanipal in Kouyunik and another palace of Sennacherib and one built by Esarhaddon in Nebi Yunas.

Nineveh's great size is attested to by the ancient geographer, Strabo; by the Greek historian, Diodorus Siculus; and by Herodotus. It appears that the four cities built by Nimrod (Genesis 10:11--12) ultimately united together and became practically one.[3] This would account for the city being about sixty miles in circumference or "a city of three days journey" (Jonah 3:3).

The atrocities of the ancient Assyrians are well known, for they boasted of them in their histories and on the bas-relief of their monuments. Ashurbanipal, the grandson of Sennacherib, was accustomed to tearing off the lips and hands of his victims. Tiglath-pilesar flayed his captives alive. Women were abused by the brutal soldiers, babies and young children were buried or burned alive, and great pyramids of human heads were made of the vanquished.[4] It is no wonder that the cries of the innocent and the cruelties

---

3. See "Nineveh," in *The Biblical World*, ed. C. F. Pfeiffer (Grand Rapids: Baker, 1966), pp. 415-21.

inflicted on the oppressed rose up before the face of God. Assyria was ripe for judgment, and a messenger of God must announce her doom.

Westward Ho!

Jonah's response to his commission is well known. He "rose up to flee to Tarshish from the presence (lit., from before the face) of Yahweh; and he went down to Joppa (modern Jaffa), found a ship which was going to Tarshish, paid the fare and went down into it to go with them to Tarshish from the presence of Yahweh" (Jonah 1:3).

Nineveh lay 500 miles northeast of Samaria where Jonah lived. Joppa (the city where, in New Testament times, Peter received the vision of the sheet let down from heaven; Acts 10) was on the coastline of the Mediterranean, and Tarshish (ancient Tartessus) was a Phoenician town in Spain 2000 miles westward.[5]

In "fleeing from the presence of the LORD," Jonah was not trying to escape God entirely. His prayer in chapter 2 shows that he was thoroughly familiar with the Scriptures and particularly the Psalms. He must have known of David's testimony when he wrote: "Where can I escape

---

4. See D. D. Luckenbill, *The Annals of Sennacherib* (Chicago: University of Chicago Press, 1924); and H. L. Oppenheim, "Babylonian and Assyrian Historical Texts," *Ancient Near Eastern Texts*, pp. 265-317.

from your Spirit? Or where can I flee from Your presence? If I ascend to heaven, You are there; if I make my bed in Sheol, again, You are there. If I take [my flight] on the wings of the dawn, or dwell in the limit of the western sea, even there Your hand will lead me, and Your right hand will hold me fast" (Psalm 139:7-10).

How then are we to explain Jonah's action? The only satisfactory answer seems to be that Jonah was "resigning" as a prophet. His love for his people, Israel, was such that he would rather turn his back on God's commission than do anything that might aid his people's enemies. He therefore chose to remove himself as far from the situation as possible.

On arriving in Joppa, Jonah just happened to find a goodly, decked vessel bound for Tarshish. It appeared to him as if the Lord was doing nothing to stop him. He paid for a one-way ticket and settled down on one of the lower decks where he went to sleep.

---

5. The ancient mariners believed that the earth was flat, and that beyond the Pillars of Hercules (known today as the Straits of Gibraltar) was the end of the world. The fact that Jonah wanted to go to Tarshish in southern Spain indicates that he was trying to get as far from Nineveh as he possibly could. In *The Mishnah* (Baba Bathra, 3:2) we read that the Jewish law allowed at least two full years for a round trip to Spain. This further signifies how remote Tarshish was from the mainstream of Hebrew life.

There is a very revealing touch in Jonah's mention of his payment of the fare for his one-way ticket. Normally, such a matter would be passed over without mention. Jonah, however, seems to be going through a typical "disobedience syndrome." He seems to be saying, "I will retain my integrity in spite of my disobedience. I will be just as good a believer in Tarshish as I was in Samaria. I will continue to honor the Lord in my life with one exception: I will not go to Nineveh."

Additional evidence of this may be gleaned from verse 10. Somewhat remorsefully, but with no thought of undoing what he had done, Jonah must have told the sailors why he was going to Tarshish. In this respect, he is like many today who feel that they can disobey God in one particular area and yet still live for Him. Quite recently one of the writers had occasion to talk to a young woman following a Sunday service. She was in the throes of divorcing her husband to marry another man. "I know I don't have biblical grounds for divorce," she said defensively, "but I believe I can still live a good Christian life even after I marry Tom." How like Jonah! And how easy to sin when we have made up our minds to take the first step away from God.

Fortunately for us (and looking at those events from the divine perspective) we can never flee from God's presence. From the human point of view, however, He follows us with an unrelenting pace. Francis Thompson described his experience in his famous poem, "The Hound of Heaven."

I fled Him, down the nights and down the days;
I fled Him, down the arches of the years;
I fled Him, down the labyrinthine ways
Of my own mind; and in the mist of tears I hid from
Him,and under running laughter.
Up vistaed hopes I sped; And shot, precipitated,
Adown Titanic glooms of chasmed fears,
From those strong Feet that followed, followed after.
But with unhurrying chase, And unperturbed pace,
Deliberate speed, majestic instancy,
They beat--and a Voice beat
More instant than the Feet--
"All things betray thee, who betrayest Me."'

Seeds of Insecurity

But the saga of Jonah contains more for us than the history of a disobedient prophet. Behind the scenes there is God, and in His relationship with His disobedient "son" there are lessons for all of us. In making His will known to Jonah, God shows us something of His personality. He is confident. He speaks with authority. He is not overbearing or harsh. Neither is He permissive. His words are challenging and direct: "Arise, go . . . cry." The imperatives contain a note of urgency (see Jonah 3:4); they constitute a call to action.

So often in our earthly relationships with our children we betray our own feelings of insecurity. This takes two primary forms. We can either command our children in such an authoritarian way that they respond out of fear, or we can plead timidly with them, ultimately destroying their respect for authority.

When we are guilty of the former, our sons and daughters grow up lacking a sound understanding of love and the way love is manifested. They will also lack the security which love creates. When this happens, their own relationships with others will betray their insecurity, for they will tend either to be fearfully passive or go to the opposite extreme and become harsh and demanding. On the other hand, when we are guilty of the latter, we fail to exercise proper authority. For example, we might say to a son, "Please do me a favor and take out the garbage." Or to a daughter, "Well, honey, I'm busy right now. Would you mind too much if I didn't practice the piano with you tonight?" These approaches may have the "Dale Carnegie touch," but they fail to show our children the strength of character and confidence in our role as parents which is so necessary if they are to grow to maturity respecting authority, exercising appropriate restraint and able to take the initiative.

All of this does not mean that we are to be autocratic. It does mean that we need to accept and exercise our God-given responsibilities and be comfortable in our role. This will communicate to our children a sense of security. In developing their own identity and personality, children test the strength of those above them in terms of authority and responsibility. This is all part of their development. When parents give directives in a weak fashion, or in an unassuming "nice guy" manner, it becomes easy for the child to lose respect for them and take commands lightly. This in turn develops sloppy attitudes and a lack of awareness of responsibility.

By following the example of God the Father, we will give our children a positive model to emulate. In giving them instruction (as God did Jonah), we should be careful to do it within the framework of our parental responsibility and assure them of the special place they have in our affections. This will breed respect, and their response to our loving authority will better prepare them for the future.

In God's words to Jonah He gave him everything he needed to know in order for his mind to enlighten his emotions so that his will could then respond appropriately. There was the call to action ("Arise"), the specific command ("go . . . cry") and the explanation ("their wickedness has come up before Me"). In dealing with us, God treats us as intelligent participants with Him in His work. He gives us authoritative commands, demonstrating His security and authority. He respects our intelligence by giving a rationale for His commands so that we need not respond in blind, uninformed faith. Furthermore, He gives us the broad parameters of His will and leaves us to work out some of the details.

One of the tragedies found in adults who have been denied the opportunity to take on appropriate responsibility during their childhood and youth is that they lack confidence. They doubt their own abilities and exhibit a fear of failure. They frequently become dependent upon others for certain skills and concentrate their energies only on the things they know they can do well. When their fear of failure is carried over into new dimensions in their lives, such as spiritual matters or the taking on of new responsibilities, they tend to take refuge behind the cliché, "I can't do anything; God must do everything." Such people need to experience with the apostle Paul the assurance that they can do all things through Christ who strengthens them (Philippians 4:13).

Fortunately for us, God knows how to work in all of our experiences to help us develop our full potential. All He asks of us is submission to His will and obedience to His Word.

Decision and Responsibility

In addition, from the way in which God dealt with Jonah we learn that He allows us certain freedom–including freedom to make mistakes, as well as disobey Him and experience the consequences. And yet, He also brings us back to Himself.

Jonah found that God's thoughts were not his thoughts. The narrative is singularly silent on any dialogue. Perhaps deep within himself Jonah had to acknowledge that God had a right to send him to Nineveh. But acting immaturely, he chose to avoid any discussion rather than voice his objections.

If this is so, then Jonah behaved as we often do. Acknowledging that God is right doesn't prevent our self-will from manifesting itself. We tend to rationalize our disobedience and then conclude that "God understands me. He knows the situation I'm in. I don't believe He will discipline me for my actions. I'll still serve Him in my own way and to the best of my ability."

How different was the experience of another prophet, Habakkuk. God spoke to him and gave him some unwelcome news (Habakkuk 1:5-11). In contrast to Jonah, Habakkuk was willing to state his concerns (1:12-17). He was also prepared to wait for God's reply (2:1). In his attitude he showed his acknowledgment of God's sovereignty, even though he could not resolve the problems associated with God's plan. His faith (2:4) helped him triumph over the enigmas of life.

Unfortunately for us, when once our hearts have begun to entertain the idea of rebelling against God--even in one small area of our lives--Satan makes it easy for us to sin. He deludes us into thinking that God is approving of our actions. As with Jonah we may find that everything seems to be falling into place. We find, as it were, a ship that just happens to be going where we want to go. When this happens we need to beware. Circumstances at best are only marginal evidence of God's will. Of primary importance is what God has revealed in His Word. Why then does God allow these circumstances to fall into place? If He is sovereign, aren't circumstances evidence of His tacit approval?

God is an all-wise Father. He allows us to make certain choices in order that we might learn the consequences of our self-will. When we do this we have the opportunity of growing toward maturity (by learning the folly of our immature impulses) and also of approving the wisdom of His plan for our lives.

A parent who is too restrictive and limits or "boxes in" his or her child's behavior may produce an "ideal" child (at home) who later does not know how to exercise either responsibility or restraint when parental authority is removed. The "walls" we build about our children should have a certain elasticity to them. Our sons and daughters should feel that they have freedom to move and express themselves. When this happens, then they will come ultimately of their own free will to approve the values and principles of their parents.

As we shall see in our next chapter, God did not withdraw from Jonah even though Jonah had withdrawn from Him. He followed His disobedient servant and, in a sovereign way, brought him back to Himself.

INTERACTION

1. What dimensions of sonship was the elder brother overlooking as he responded to his father (see Luke 15:29)? What are some possible dimensions of being a child of God that we might lose sight of, and how might these oversights limit the fullness of our own Christian experience?

2. In what ways may we be tempted to be intolerant or judgmental of others in a manner similar to the elder brother? How is this illustrated by Jonah's response to God's commission?

3. What are some of the situations your child/children might be facing where your reassurance would be important to their feelings of security?

4. Betty and Jack Smith have a seven-year-old son, Robbie. For reasons of health, Betty has been unable to have additional children and the Smith's have been discussing the possibility of adopting a boy between the ages of five and six to be a playmate for Robbie and to fill out their family circle. Sensitive to the needs of all children for feelings of love, security, belonging and confidence, both Betty and Jack are looking carefully at their own capacity to meet these needs for both Robbie and his new brother. In light of the principles discussed in this chapter, what are some of the issues and challenges of which parents will need to be aware and are likely to face? What are some of the problems or difficulties you,

as a parent, might be facing in which, by sharing your concerns with one another, you may receive encouragement and support from fellow parents (see Ephesians 6:1-4)?

NOTES

Chapter 3

CAN WE RUN AWAY FROM GOD?

As the congregation was leaving church one morning and the pastor was receiving the usual comments on his sermon, a young woman asked if she might speak to him. He agreed and she waited. The woman's husband was a traveling salesman, and she was left to rear their young son alone.

When the crowd of churchgoers had dispersed, the minister came to where the young woman was standing in the shade of a tree on the patio. "How may I help you?" he asked.

"It's my son, Bobby," she said hesitatingly. "When his father is not at home, he thinks he can do as he pleases. The other day he was very disobedient and I spanked him. A friend arrived just as I finished and, of course, heard Bobby crying. She then told me that spanking him would warp his personality. Pastor, what shall I do? Will discipline 'warp his personality'? Will it turn him against me?"

This young mother's dilemma is by no means unique. The problem of how to discipline our children faces all of us at one time or another.

A Thorny Problem

Advice on the subject of discipline runs the gamut from an extremely harsh, authoritarian kind on the one hand, to a very permissive, lax model on the other. In recent years two psychologists, Rudolph Dreikers and Loren Grey, have advocated a "family democracy." Their book, *A New Approach to Discipline*, illustrates how their theory may be applied. One of the illustrations they use centers in a home where there are three teenage girls. One day, at a family council meeting, the girls announced that inasmuch as they constituted a majority they were going to establish their own rules regarding the frequency of their dates and how late they stayed up. They also stated that they fail to see why they should be required to call home to inform their parents where they are and when they will return. As can be expected, their parents were unhappy with this decision and their mother argued against the stand they had taken. The girls, however, were adamant and their parents were overruled.

To show their daughters the fallacy of their thinking, the mother decided to demonstrate the undemocratic nature of their decision. A few days later, having told no one but her husband, she left home to spend the night with a friend. She did not advise her daughters of her plans, make preparations for the evening meal, or call home to tell them where she was.

When the mother in the story did return home, it was to find her teenage daughters in a state of agitation. They were angry with her and quickly demanded where she had been and why she did not tell them of her plans. "At the last family council meeting," the mother reminded them, "you voted to go out when you pleased, and to stay out as long as you liked without notifying anyone of where you were going, or when you would return."

Well, according to Drs. Dreikers and Grey, the next family meeting was conducted in a totally different manner. The girls had came to realize the need for mutual consideration and the importance in a democracy of exercising responsibility as well as restraint. But what of those families (and, regrettably, they are in the majority) where parents do not have the wisdom, skill or patience to teach their children consistently the importance of responsibility and restraint at all levels of their growth?

In the way we rear our sons and daughters, freedom should be balanced by certain controls, and liberty should be counterpoised by a consideration of others. Unfortunately for us, problems over discipline remain. Sometimes they even divide the home. On the one hand, a father may feel the need to discipline his child only to be opposed by his wife; and on the other, there are those instances where a wife may look to her husband to discipline the children only to find that he leaves everything to her. And even if parents are in agreement over the need for discipline, the decision still must be made on the most appropriate method to be employed.

In this connection, it is interesting to notice how God dealt with Jonah who, though a mature young man, in his disobedience retrogressed to an adolescent state of rebellion (Jonah 1:4-16).

Bones of Contention

When Jonah left Samaria for Joppa (Jonah 1:4-16) he just happened to find a ship bound for Tarshish. He was glad to obtain a berth, and either at the time of boarding the vessel or while waiting for the ship to set sail, told the sailors (perhaps in answer to their question about his long voyage) the reason for his journey to Tarshish. [1]

In due time the vessel put out to sea, and Jonah went down to one of the lower decks to rest. Before they had gone very far from land, the Lord hurled a great wind upon the sea. The strong gusts developed into a succession of mighty squalls, and the sailors (the Hebrew text calls them "old salts") became afraid. They were experienced mariners, and had witnessed firsthand the Mediterranean's many

---

1. The Hebrew text of verse 3 implies that Jonah was fleeing from his standing as a prophet before Yahweh. He was, in effect, resigning as God's servant. This, however, he could not do, for having at one time voluntarily submitted himself to the authority of the Lord, he could not now go back on his commitment.

changing moods. In all the storms they had encountered, however, none had ever been as boisterous as this one. The ship was tossed about, and every wave they crested plunged them into an abyss from which they expected never to emerge.

To give buoyancy to the vessel, the sailors jettisoned the cargo. But the waves continued to beat so heavily against the sides of the ship that at any moment they expected the boards to give way. In their extremity, these hardened seamen resorted to prayer and each cried out to his god(s). Ironically, the "god of the storm," commonly worshiped throughout the ancient world at this time, was Baal.[2] If he was even then riding on the clouds and discharging his thunderbolts, then surely he would hear their earnest entreaties.

The prayers of the sailors were of no avail, and in desperation the captain went in search of Jonah. To his astonishment, he found the prophet asleep. His words were harsh: "How is it that you are sleeping [at such a time as this]? Get up! Call on your God. Perhaps He[3] will be concerned about us so that we will not perish!"

---

2. See A. S. Kapelrud, *Baal in the Ras Shamra Texts* (Copenhagen: Gad, 1952), pp. 93ff.
3. The Hebrew text contains the article with the word 'Elohim, implying "the [true] God." This contrasts sharply with the false gods who, so far, have proved powerless to help them.

But why was Jonah asleep? Wouldn't the unusual motion of the boat rising up, and then like a rollercoaster, plunging downward- have awakened him? The best answer seems to be that his deep sleep was a defense against what he has done. In his determination to disobey the Lord he had, in effect, turned his back on everything that had characterized his life up to this time. This included the way in which he had been reared, his preparation for the ministry, and his service as a prophet.

In all probability, he had rationalized his disobedience to satisfy his mental anxieties. But he could not quiet the misgivings of his heart, and the more his conscience plagued him, the more he attempted to reason his way out of his predicament. The truth, however, was all too plain. He could not follow God in the general course of his life and be disobedient to Him in one of the specifics. Wearied by the constant tension between his thought processes and his emotional misgivings, he sought release in sleep. The depth of his slumber was in all probability a psychological defense against his emotional trauma.

We cannot help but wonder about Jonah's response to the captain when he awakened him and asked him to pray. The prophet knew instinctively why the storm had come upon them. He also knew that there was no use praying unless he was ready to repent of his sin and go to Nineveh. In this respect he was in a similar situation to many Christians today. Our nation, our society, our church, and our homes are beset by grave problems. The responsibility of every believer should be earnest entreaty that the Lord will be gracious to us and help us. Instead, it is a terrible indictment of us that secular leaders have to challenge us to pray.

Unmasked

Perhaps it is while the captain is below with Jonah that the sailors, in desperation, decided to cast lots to determine who is responsible for the storm. The custom of casting lots was widespread in the ancient Near East (cf. Nehemiah 11:l; Proverbs 16:33; Acts 1:23,26). It was done in Old Testament times to determine the will of God (or the gods). It is not practiced by believers in the church today because we have the mind of Christ (1 Corinthians 2:16), and the Holy Spirit indwells us and guides us into all truth (John 14:16, 17, 26; 16:13). In the case of Jonah, however, the casting of lots served to unmask him. And once identified as the culprit, the sailors began to interrogate him.

"What have you done to bring this calamity on us?" one asks.

"And what is your occupation?" inquires another.

"Where do you come from?" interjects a third.

"What is your country? [And] from what people are you?" interposes a fourth member of the crew.

The questioning is purposeful, and it is done with fairness and impartiality. The sailors are not prepared to condemn the prophet without giving him every opportunity to explain the cause of the storm. Behind these questions lie certain accepted assumptions that people in those days used to explain why the gods might pursue a person in order to punish him. Had he committed some sin for which he had not atoned? Was his occupation displeasing to one of the local deities? Had he passed through a country and committed a crime for which he was now being punished? Or was it possible that the gods had a vendetta against all people of his race? The goal of the sailors was to find out why a rankled deity might even now be punishing them for this prophet's misdeeds.

Jonah's response to these questions is clear and direct. His answer is also a testimony to the greatness, power and glory of the One whom he serves. "I am a Hebrew," he says, "and I worship Yahweh (the LORD), God[4] of heaven, who made the sea and the dry land." While Jonah does not answer all the specifics of the sailors' questions, his confession is sufficient to remind them of his former statement that he was fleeing from the Lord. The sailors now realize that his God is more than a tribal deity, and this knowledge fills them with reverential awe.

---

4. Once again the Hebrew text contains the article with 'Elohim, implying the only true God in contrast to gods of wood or stone that could not help the sailors in their predicament.

Prisoners of Conscience

But what can they do? They are caught between a disobedient prophet and an all-powerful God. And He, as a Parent, must deal with His child's disobedience. In desperation they turn to Jonah and ask, "What shall we do to you that the sea may be calm to us?" To this question the rebellious prophet replies, "Pick me up and throw me into the sea; then the storm will cease for I know that on my account this great storm has come upon you."

The sailors, however, are more righteous in their response than is the messenger of the Lord. They exhibit an unusual appreciation of the sanctity of human life and row hard (lit., "dig" their oars into the sea, 1:13) in an endeavor to bring the ship to land. But their efforts are of no avail. The storm only increases in strength. Finally, in desperation they pray to Jonah's God[5], the covenant God of Israel: "We earnestly pray, 0 LORD (i.e., Yahweh), do not let us perish on account of this man's life and do not put innocent blood on us; for as You willed You have done." Then they throw Jonah overboard. Immediately the sea stops its raging and the sailors offer a sacrifice[6] to the Lord and make vows. Through Jonah's unwitting witness they have come to know the true God and readily submit to His authority.

---

5. By praying to Yahweh, these sailors were, in effect, turning their backs on their gods. See 2 Kings 5 where Naaman renounced the gods of Syria when he immersed himself in the River Jordan.

It is significant that the vows are made after the storm ceases. Many people make vows in a crisis only to forget them after the pressure of the moment has passed. These sailors, however, show the reality of their profession by obligating themselves to do something after God has removed the threat (cf. Psalm 68:19).

In all of this we see once again God's interest in His creatures. All are important to Him. We also observe how He uses events and circumstances to bring people to Himself. He makes even the disobedience of a rebellious prophet the means of bringing light and understanding to Gentile seamen (cf. 2 Peter 3:9).

Jonah, however, is still rebellious. He prefers drowning to going to Nineveh. He believes that by being thrown overboard he will thwart the purpose of God. God, however, has prepared "A Maritime Connection" for Jonah and, as we shall see in our next chapter, He eventually brings him to the point of submission to His authority

Reason and Responsibility

In applying the teaching of these verses to the problems of parenting, we notice first that God, as an all-wise, all-

---

6. The word used is *zebach* and is used of a sacrifice with or without blood. It differs from *'olah*, the term which, in the course of time, became the accepted term for a sacrifice involving the shedding of blood.

powerful Father, allows us freedom of choice. As the story shows, He controls everything (e.g., the storm) except our wills. He has chosen to limit Himself in this area in order that we may glorify Him by our willing obedience.

In rearing our children we frequently find ourselves in a power struggle for their wills. To bring about behavior that is pleasing to us, we sometimes resort to manipulation: "I'll let you go to Elizabeth's home after school if you will do this for me." Or, "I'll let you have the car tonight if you will promise to go to church on Sunday."

It is interesting to notice that God did not manipulate Jonah into obedience. He allowed him to go to Joppa, pay for a one-way ticket, and actually set sail for Tarshish. Jonah knew that he had committed himself to the lifelong service of the Lord. He had voluntarily submitted to God's sovereignty. The Lord was, therefore, entitled to his obedience. Even in disciplining His prophet, God allowed him freedom of choice. At no time did He deprive him of his autonomy. This is obvious, for in speaking to the sailors Jonah chose drowning ("throw me overboard") to repentance.

It is also worth observing that the almighty God was sensitive to the needs of the sailors and the strength of the ship. The storm increased in strength only when God willed it (Jonah 1:13). The men thought that at any moment the ship would be broken to pieces, but God was responsive to their situation (Jonah 1:4). He did not use excessive force.

The sides of the ship held. Throughout the storm His grace and longsuffering were in evidence. He was leading them to repentance (cf. Romans 2:4,5).

As a result of the storm the sailors became acutely aware of their need. In their extremity they prayed "each man to his god." This was their response to their newly aroused feeling of fear (i.e., insecurity). And God did not test them beyond their ability. He brought them to see the insufficiency of their efforts and their pagan beliefs, and then led them through the crisis to faith and trust in Himself.

In a similar way, parents need to be sensitive to the trauma their children face in the crises of life. The danger of our insensitivity is very real. As parents, we need to be aware of this and be on our guard against ignoring our children's fears or minimizing their anxieties. By far the best course of action for us to follow is to encourage them to recognize their fears and then place their confidence in the One who is Master of the storms of life (cf. 1 Corinthians 10:13; 1 Peter 5:7).

Handling Disobedience

In addition to allowing our children freedom of choice, we also need to know how to deal with them when they are disobedient. In this connection, it is instructive to see how God handled Jonah. While not limiting the prophet in any way, He did discipline him. And the discipline (i.e., the storm) lasted only until Jonah made a decision. Oftentimes our discipline is not corrective but coercive. We apply the Bible's teaching about "sparing the rod and spoiling the child" (see Proverbs 10:13; 13:24; 22:15; etc.) indiscriminately, and forget the apostle Paul's warning "not to embitter our children, lest they become discouraged" (Colossians 3:21). Our discipline is frequently an outlet for our own frustration. To be sure, God disciplined Jonah. He did not respond to Jonah's regression to adolescent rebellion with a similar pattern of behavior. Instead, He handled Jonah's stubbornness with patience, his anger with love, and his defiance of His authority with forbearance. He was then able to deal with His rebellious prophet consistently and without compromising His position.

In this connection, we have a great deal to learn from our heavenly Father. In the same way that God dealt with Jonah's unreasonableness and refusal to respond to authority antithetically (i.e., with patience and understanding as opposed to stubbornness and an unwillingness to listen to reason), even so we may handle our sons and daughters. In addition, even as God did not demand perfection from Jonah, neither should we expect perfection from our children.

Finally, from God the Father's example in Jonah 1, we learn that a parent must so love a child (even while disciplining him or her) that the child feels secure in his parent's love even while being disciplined.

INTERACTION

1. Why do people pray in times of crisis? In your response, carefully consider the inner feelings as opposed to simply the outer circumstances. How can we, as parents, lead our children to a consistent pattern of trust in God, as opposed to simply calling upon Him in times of trial?

2. A group of school children were asked to give their definition of the word "discipline." One little fellow replied, "Discipline is something unpleasant that happened to Daddy when he was young." Perhaps many of us can readily identify with this father's experience, but is it possible, in light of the implication raised by his son's definition, that our own children may not be experiencing an appropriate level of discipline in their own lives? Why is discipline necessary in bringing a child to full maturity?

3. What are the principles concerning discipline that you have been able to glean from reading of this chapter? List them and then discuss ways to implement them.

4. What are some of the reasons why fathers might be hesitant to give leadership in the disciplining of their children? May some of them also be felt by the mothers?

5. How may we be sure that the way in which we discipline our children is truly geared toward helping our children as opposed to merely giving vent to our own anger and frustration?

NOTES

Chapter 4

THE MARITIME CONNECTION

Some years ago a young farm boy asked his mother, "Where did the cow get her baby?" The lad's favorite heifer had just given birth to a calf. The young boy's mother, taken aback by the suddenness of the question, replied: "Oh, she found it under a bush in the pasture." With that she sent her son off to occupy himself elsewhere.

As the young lad grew to manhood, he reflected more than once on what his mother had told him. To be sure, the cow that had first caused him to question where baby calves come from had been put out to pasture with the other livestock that morning. It is also possible that, in the heat of the day and feeling that the time of delivery was drawing near, she lay down in the shade of a tree and there gave birth. That evening, after licking her calf clean, she returned to the stable with her offspring following on wobbly legs behind her.

The mother's reply, however, was a deliberate attempt to evade an honest question, and many parents before and since have resorted to the same kind of strategy. Their answer may "get them off the hook" temporarily, but it fails to satisfy the inquirer and destroys the trust, which should exist between a child and his parent.[1]

---

1. In the Hebrew Bible, chapter 1 ends with verse 16. Verse 17 is, therefore, logically connected with chapter 2.

How different with God the Father. He tells us what we need to know without ambiguity to cloud the issues. In our present passage, and with marvelous economy of words, He explains to us what happened to Jonah when he was swallowed by a great fish. What He tells us may stretch our minds, but it has the ring of truth to it. And as we mature, we have the opportunity of investigating matters further to learn more of the marvels of His providence.

As Christian parents, we should do well to model ourselves after our heavenly Father. We should answer our children's questions honestly and teach them with mind-expanding information. In the early stages of their search for knowledge, brief answers are best. These need not go beyond the satisfaction of their curiosity. Then, as our children grow older, they will be able to develop their own interests and build upon what we have taught them. Further questions will then deserve more complete answers.

A Case in Point

The people of Jonah's day would readily believe what was recounted to them. Sailors, plying their trade up and down the Mediterranean, had for centuries brought back stories of amazing sea creatures--whales, sharks, and manta rays. They did not have terms to describe these monsters of the deep, but the stories they related (while probably exaggerated) were readily believed. God's dealings with Jonah, while devoid of exaggeration, nevertheless would be accepted by those who heard it. And we, from our perspective, and knowing more about marine biology than they did, can divide creatures of the animal kingdom into *phyla* for further study. With this knowledge we can better understand what happened to Jonah.

Intellectual Ferment

Critics, however, have always pointed to the book of Jonah as evidence of the unscientific or fictional character of the Bible. With a flamboyant display of sophistication, they assure us that the story of "Jonah and the Whale" is pure myth. To substantiate their point, they inform us that whales have very small throats, live largely on plankton and strain out larger fish, which might be caught in their mouths. Then, to try and make it easier for Bible-believing Christians to accept their position, they point to pagan literature current at the time and assert that this account is merely a Jewish parallel to the story of Andromeda and Perseus,[2] or Hesione and Hercules.[3]

In answering these assertions we need to consider first the kind of "sea creature" that swallowed Jonah. The Hebrew text records that it was an *adol*, "great fish," but

---

2. Cf. C. A. Avery, ed., *The New Century Handbook of Greek Mythology and Legend* (New York: Appleton-Century-Crofts, 1972), pp.52-53.
3. Ibid., pp. 282-83.

does not specify what kind. When the Lord Jesus referred to this incident in Matthew 12:40, He employed the noun *ketos*, "sea monster," to describe the creature that ingested Jonah. He did not use the usual word for fish, *ichthus*. This has led some writers to adopt the view that Jonah was, in fact, swallowed by the *Rhineodon* or whale shark. This unique species attains the size as big as some whales and has a mouth large enough to swallow several men standing shoulder to shoulder.[4]

We should not, however, dismiss the idea that Jonah may have been swallowed by a Cachelot (or sperm) whale known to inhabit the Mediterranean. Those who wish to cast aspersion on the reliability of Jonah's experience provide data only for those whales (*e.g.*, the right whale) where the swallowing of a man would be impossible. The sperm whale, however, has a mouth and throat wide enough to admit several men and, in contrast to its plankton-eating northern cousin, feeds on giant squid.[5] When dying, it also

---

4. A small "whale shark" is on display in the Vanderbilt Museum, Long Island, NY. For further information, see the *Encyclopedia Briticannica* (1966), XX: 4-75; Thor Hyerdahl's *Kon Tiki* (New York: Rand McNally, 1960), pp. 120-21; and Jacques Yves Cousteau's *The Ocean World of Jacques Cousteau* (New York: Abrams, 1974), in which he recounts the "tagging" of a whale shark in the Mediterranean. Further corroboration of the possibility of a man being swallowed by one of these sharks may be obtained from *The Daily Mail*, Birmingham, England, December 14, 1928; and the *Madras* (India) *Mail*, November 28, 1946.

ejects from its stomach undigested food. This fact is borne out by a ship's captain, Frank T. Bullen, who, in *The Cruise of the Cachalot*, records how a sperm whale was speared by men of his crew and disgorged pieces of cuttle fish eight feet square (cf. Jonah 2:10).[6] Furthermore, being an air-breathing mammal, Jonah could have lived in its dark interior without asphyxiating.

The fact that Jonah was preserved "three days and three nights" in the belly of this "fish" receives incidental testimony from another whaling expedition. The ship, *Star of the East*, sighted a sperm whale in the vicinity of the Falkland Islands. Two boats were launched to help spear the whale. When attacked, the whale upset one boat and one of the men was drowned. His mate, James Bartley, disappeared. After the whale had been killed, it was drawn alongside the ship and the whalers set about removing the blubber. They worked all day and part of the night. The next

---

5. The sperm whale swims with its mouth open and the skin of its lower jaw swells out (similar to that of a snake swallowing prey larger than itself), see *Bibliotheca Sacra* LXXII (1915), pp. 336ff.; *Encyclopedia Britannica* (1966), XXII:554ff.; Herman Melville's *Moby Dick* (New York: Dodd, Mead, n.d.), pp. 303-07; and Frank T. Bullen's *Cruise of the Cachalot* (New York: Grossett and Dunlap, 1923), pp. 77, 191, 221, 342, etc.
6. Additional evidence may be obtained from Sir John Bland Sutton's presidential address, "A Lecture on the Psychology of Animals Being Swallowed Alive," Royal College of Surgeons, London; and Sir Francis Fox's *Sixty-three Years of Engineering* (London: Murray, 1924), pp. 295-300.

morning they were startled by spasmodic signs of life inside the stomach. In cutting through the walls of the stomach, they found James Bartley--a raving lunatic. He was washed down with seawater and confined to the captain's quarters. At the end of three weeks, he had recovered from his shock and was able to resume his duties.[7]

When questioned about his experience, Bartley stated that when thrown from the boat he remembers being "encompassed by a great darkness" and "slipping along a smooth passage of some sort. The sensation lasted for a short term and then I realized I had more room. I felt about me and my hands came into contact with a yielding slimy substance that seemed to shrink from my touch. It finally dawned on me what had happened. I could breathe easily, but the heat [104-106 degrees Fahrenheit] was terrible . . . It

---

7. Similar testimony is to be found in Fox's work cited above. The veracity of this incident was denied by Mrs. J. F. Whitney, wife of the Captain of the *Star of the East*, and her denial was brought before the Christian public by A. Lukyn Williams in *The Expository Times* (1906 and 1907). Mrs. Whitney has since been refuted by the science editor of *Journal des Debats*, Paris, Msr. DeParville, whose investigation was particularly thorough. Inasmuch as Mrs. Whitney's denial stands alone, her statement requires corroboration before it can be given serious consideration. Incidents of men being swallowed by whales have been reported in other journals and newspapers, *e.g., Neue Lutheranische Kirchenzeitun* (1985), p. 103; and "Marshal Jenkins and the Whale," *Massachusetts Gazette, Boston Post Boy and Advertiser*, No. 738, Monday, October 14, 1771.

seemed to open the pores of my skin and draw out the vitality."

James Bartley's skin was bleached by the gastric juices in the whale's stomach to a deadly whiteness (cf. Luke 11:29-30) and took on the appearance of parchment. On being asked how long he thought he could have survived, Bartley replied: "Until I starved."

While we do not need to come to any final decision as to whether Jonah was swallowed by a whale,[8] a *Rhineodon* shark or some other sea creature, these incidents prove beyond question that such occurrences have happened and that the people concerned survived. There is nothing in all of modern research to cause us to disbelieve the record of Jonah and the "whale."

In the light of these historic facts, what are we to make of the assertion that the account of Jonah being swallowed by a "sea monster" is a Jewish counterpart of a pagan myth?

The legend of Andromeda and Perseus, and the lesser-known story of Hesione and Hercules, bear similar characteristics to one another which are missing in the biblical nar-

---

8. No real distinction in terminology was made by the ancient Hebrews to differentiate between large sharks and sea mammals. The term "sea monster" was used of sharks, manta rays, and whales. Cf. *Zondervan's Pictorial Encyclopedia of the Bible*, V:925.

rative. In both accounts, the sea god, Poseidon, was angered and wrought destruction on the land. To satisfy his capricious nature, a beautiful girl was to be chained to some rocks, there to await the incoming tide, at which time she would be eaten by a sea monster. In both accounts she was saved by her hero-lover and afterwards became his wife. Those who see a parallel between these fanciful tales and the story of Jonah are possessed by a lively imagination that stains one's credulity. To our minds the biblical story needs no vindication. Historic facts lift it above the realm of allegory, fiction or myth.[9]

Nuggets of Wisdom

The biblical text says, "And *Yahweh* (the LORD) appointed a great fish to swallow Jonah." In the light of the foregoing, this statement is most revealing. While the Authorized Version translates *manah*, "prepared," the word carries the idea of "to appoint, ordain," and it should not be confused with special acts of creation.[10] The Jewish rabbis

---

9. Christ bore witness to the literalness of Jonah's experience in Matthew 12:39-40 and Luke 11:29-30. It would have been ludicrous for Him to say, "even as the mythical (or allegorical) Jonah was three days and three nights in the belly of the mythical (or allegorical) sea monster, even so I will spend three days and three nights in the bowels of the earth." The entire context of both passages demands that the experience of Jonah be literal. For the contrary point of view, see *The Universal Jewish Encyclopedia* (1942), VI:177.

believed that this specific fish was brought into being when God made the world and held it in readiness for Jonah. While this is improbable, considering the millennia that had intervened, it does remind us of the character of God. Beyond all doubt, in eternity past, He foresaw this contingency and planned for it (Genesis 1:21). And at the right moment He led the fish to be in the place where it could swallow Jonah.

As we study the text, we cannot help but link God's providence with His power and greatness. His control over His creatures is absolute. He caused the fish to pass through the "paths of the sea" to fulfill His will (Psalm 8:8). Scientists are only now beginning to fathom the mysteries of the deep, and yet God has had "His path in the great waters" (Psalm 77:19) since the beginning of time.

All of this should be of great encouragement to us, for God sees, knows and controls things that are far beyond our comprehension. His wisdom and power are infinite, and it is comforting for us to trust in His sovereignty in all the circumstances of our lives. The fact that He can appoint a fish to do His bidding and accomplish His purpose should encourage us as we look about us and contemplate the events that we are called upon to face day by day. He is in

---

10. Cf. *A Hebrew and English Lexicon of the Old Testament*, F. Brown, S. R. Driver, and C. A. Briggs, eds. (Oxford: Clarendon, 1962), p. 584. The term *manah,* "to appoint," differs from *asah,* "to make" or *bara,* "to create" (see Genesis 1:21).

control of these circumstances and continues to order all things for our good (cf. Romans 8:28).

But how may a fallible human parent pattern himself after an infallible, all wise heavenly Father?

In this connection, the well-known statement of Solomon may be of some help to us. He wrote, "Train up a child in the way [or, according to the way] he should go and when he is old he will not depart from it" (Proverbs 22:6). This truth is as pertinent to us now as it was when Solomon wrote it. The way we rear our children should be in accordance with their nature; the manner of their training should be in keeping with their particular characteristics and interests; and the method we use should vary with their mental and physical development. Unfortunately for our children, from the crib to graduation from college, we are content if they are either quiet or taking interest in our interests. For example, during the first few years of life, we are happy if they lie quietly in their playpen with a bottle. We become frustrated when they cry, for then we must leave what we are doing and attend to them. As our children grow, we are content if they play with their toys or watch television. We seldom take the initiative to explore their world and encourage them in keeping with their particular stage of development. This results in our children frequently being reared in three "worlds"-- (1) the sterile setting of being left to themselves, (2) the often detrimental world of television, which involves them only as passive "sponges" to absorb whatever they view, and (3) the encounters they have outside the home which bear a direct relationship to the community in which they are being reared.

In light of all of this, Horace Bushnell's observation takes on new significance. He said, "Let every Christian father and mother understand, when their child is three years old, that they have done more than half of all they will ever do for his character." The challenge to each one of us as we read about God's involvement with Jonah is to cultivate an expanding environment for those whose nurture has been entrusted to our care. While the facts given are brief, they allow us to enlarge our understanding as we learn more of God's ways with His people. We are encouraged to "dig" into His Word and develop a biblical philosophy of life for ourselves. Having learned of Him, we may then lead our children in the development of a strong God-consciousness of their own so that they may learn how to apply the principles of Scripture to the different situations they face.

To do this effectively, we should study our children individually so that we know how best to influence them for the Lord. This will require patience, the ability to pace ourselves according to their interests and rate of growth, and perseverance when results seem minimal. It also will require a determined commitment on our part--a commitment to involvement!

Parents, Beware

But then there is the tricky matter of discipline. When should we administer discipline? How severe should it be? And of what duration?

Notice, if you will, God's dealings with Jonah. Discipline could have been avoided if Jonah had been prepared to discuss how he felt openly and honestly with the Lord. This would have led (as it did with Habakkuk, cf. Habakkuk1:1--2:1) to a clarification of the issues and submission to the all-wise will of God. Instead, with an absence of dialog, Jonah left Samaria with the intention of putting as much distance between himself and Nineveh as possible. This was an act of flagrant disobedience. When he embarked for Tarshish, the Lord sent a terrific storm on the sea. The sailors confronted him, and Jonah had to admit that the storm was his fault (Jonah 1:12). But he was unwilling to repent. He believed that he could thwart the plan of God by drowning. This was a further act of willful rebellion.

Having stubbornly refused to respond to God's gentler method of discipline, Jonah now found himself in a most uncomfortable position--the hot, dark, slimy belly of a fish. He had nowhere to go, and even in that situation it took considerable time before he was willing to submit his will to the will of his Father (Jonah 2:1).

But what may we learn from God's chastisement of His recalcitrant prophet?

When we compare God's method of discipline with our own, we find that there are four basic disciplinary situations that elicit four different responses:

1. All too often our approach to our child's actions tends to be more of *an emotional reaction to his behavior* rather than a balanced, rational response. We have a tendency when provoked to respond in anger. The result is first fear and then resentment on the part of our child. We frequently fail to realize that our child's behavior has probably been triggered by his felt need for power. This need for power probably stems from a lack of confidence and his overt behavior is designed to make up for this lack.

2. If, however, we are hurt by our child's conduct, it may indicate that our child is seeking revenge. He may be feeling an acute sense of loss or injury. He may not have been able to express his feelings, or he may blame us for them. In any event, by hurting someone else he hopes to ease his own injured emotions.

3. There are also times when our reaction to our child's behavior is one of frustration. This may result from the fact that he feels the need to withdraw from active participation with life because our demands on him have been too great. His action, therefore, is an endeavor to protect himself.

4. And then there are times when our child's actions draw from us very little emotional response beyond annoyance, or may even appear amusing. This may indicate nothing more than the fact that our child wants attention. However, if we respond weakly, he may lose out on an important learning experience.

Unfortunately for our children, in matters of discipline, we rely very heavily on our emotions of anger, loss, frustration or resentment; and we mete out discipline accordingly. If, however, we pattern ourselves after our heavenly Father's example, we will be able to move away from these reactive extremes to a position of mature, balanced judgment. We will not respond from the level of our feelings, but will combine logic and discernment with our emotions in determining a proper course of action. This will result in discipline--not to induce fear or conformity, but to bring about a willing response on the part of our child.

In the case before us, God's response to Jonah's recalcitrance could have been one of anger. Jonah's conduct was characterized by disobedience, persistent rebellion and finally by total rejection of God's authority. *He was in a power struggle* with God and wanted sole control of his life. Seeing Jonah act in this way could have moved God to anger and a demonstration of His omnipotence. As a finite creature, Jonah could have been crushed before God's infinite power. Instead, the Lord tempered the storm (His initial act of discipline), while allowing Jonah to feel the consequences of his rebellious attitude and actions. This gave Jonah the opportunity to repent. Only when he chose to end his life by drowning did God intervene.

In all of this we see God's wisdom. He allowed Jonah freedom to test the boundaries of His will. Instead of severe restrictions, Jonah found that there was a degree of elasticity. The restraint imposed upon him was always with a view to bringing him back to what God knew to be best for him. For God to have yielded to Jonah's stubbornness would have given the prophet a false sense of confidence. Instead, God allowed him to struggle for power, knowing that out of this struggle would come submission and dependability.

Throughout the account we find that God dealt with Jonah from the position of strength--the strength of character with which He also deals with us. At no time was He caught off guard. In this respect, He sets parents an example to so study the nature and temperament of their sons and daughters, and to become so involved with them in their development that they, too, may know instinctively what the needs of their children are and how to meet them. And when discipline is needed, they will then be able to respond appropriately with actions that are based upon knowledge and discernment.

INTERACTION

1. Are there certain "sticky" questions your own child/children may ask that you might share with the group? Discuss how these questions might be answered appropriately at various levels of your children's development.

2. Why do skeptics have such difficulty accepting the story of Jonah and the "whale?" What evidence might you use to support your position concerning Jonah's account? If we find ourselves tending always to seek logical, natural explanations for apparent biblical miracles, where may such a tendency lead us relative to our foundations of faith? What is the difference between sound reason and enlightened faith? From what premise does God the Father operate in His dealings with us?

3. As we consider the fact of God's often quiet working behind the scenes of human experience, we are brought face to face with the fact of His sovereignty. Have there been experiences in your own life that you can look back on now and recognize His loving involvement? What is our Father's goal in intervening in our life-experience? How can we reconcile the painful circumstances we encounter (such as disaster, accident or severe illness) with the fact of God's loving care in light of His goal for us?

4. A CASE STUDY: Doris and John found themselves positively delighted with their daughter, Becky. She was attractive and charming and in every way a model child. Her every action appeared to be motivated by concern for others, for what would be helpful and constructive and for what would please her parents whom she dearly loved. Becky tended to present the slightest trace of shyness as opposed to being free and outgoing, and this characteristic seemed only to add to her charm. Occasionally, however, when Doris would ask something of Becky, she would be aware of a bit of stubbornness or even a hint of rebellion in her daughter's response. This occurred so infrequently, however, that Doris seldom gave it a second thought.

When Becky was 17 years old, her behavior suddenly changed. Her relationship with her parents, and particularly her mother, rapidly deteriorated. This brought much anguish to Doris' heart. This pattern of behavior continued for a considerable period of time and resulted in much soul-searching on the part of Doris and John. "Where had they gone wrong? What had they done to cause Becky's drastic change to a hostile, acting-out young adult?"

Doris and John sought the aid of a counselor and were helped to recognize Becky's great need for security in their love and confidence in her own worth and adequacy. They began to understand the significance of her "charm" and "goodness" as a strong attempt to earn parental approval and her "shyness" as an indication of her insecurity. Furthermore, they began to appreciate the early hints of stubbornness and rebellion as evidence of the building hostility, and her struggle for her own identity as an acceptable and lovable person, regardless of her behavior.

In what specific ways might Doris and John have become tuned in to Becky's needs and patterns of growth and, in keeping with Proverbs 22:6, provided reassurance of their love and personal affirmation? What principles do you find in the last portion of the chapter that would also have been a help to Becky's parents?

NOTES

Chapter 5

THE DEPTHS OF DELIVERANCE

Strides in communication now permit us to talk with people half-way around the world, and e-mail messages have replaced the letter as a favorite method of passing along information. In spite of these advantages, we still have difficulty bridging the gap within our families. Open interaction necessitates that those in our homes freely share their thoughts and feelings, ideals and disappointments with us. Good communication has always been a two-way street.

In the case before us, it was Jonah who broke off communication with God the Father (Jonah 1). The result was a vain attempt on Jonah's part to deny the Lord His rightful place in his life. His stubborn self-will blocked all interaction. He was out of the will of God, and he knew it. When confronted with his sin, he preferred drowning to yielding his will to the Lord.

The Flawed Escape

But Jonah did not drown (Jonah 1:17—2:1).[1] Strong currents must have pulled him downward, and in their grip

---

1. In the Hebrew Bible chapter 1 ends with verse 16. Jonah 1:17 logically belongs with chapter 2.

he was powerless. Those who have been near to drowning know that their inability to struggle against a powerful undertow fills them with fear. The pressure of the water on their ears causes intense pain. Their audible heartbeats, pounding like a trip-hammer in their temples, become deafening. Lights begin to flash before their eyes, and their lungs feel as if they will burst. Flashes of recollection appear on the screen of memory--and all this in the moments before they yield to the inevitable and a merciful unconsciousness.

In *Richard III,* Shakespeare has the Duke of Clarence describe his experience. He says:

> Lord! Lord! me thought, what pain it was to drown!
> What dreadful noise of waters in mine ears!
> What ugly sights of death within mine eyes!

And such undoubtedly was Jonah's experience (Jonah 2:2-7). In his extremity, "while he was fainting away," he called out to the Lord.[2] This cry constituted his first faltering step towards restoring communication. His prayer was immediately heard by God in His Temple, and Jonah was

---

2. The entire prayer recorded in Jonah 2 was prayed in the belly of the fish. Verses 4-7, however, describe an earlier experience and Jonah's reminiscences before being swallowed by the fish which the Lord had appointed to "bring him up from the pit." Cf. E. J. Young, *An Introduction to the Old Testament* (Grand Rapids: Eerdmans, 1960), pp. 281-82.

swallowed by the "sea monster" that the Lord had appointed for the purpose.

No Compromise

In recounting his experience (and with his amanuensis dutifully recording every word), Jonah says, "And I was in the stomach of the fish three days and three nights.[3] Then I prayed to the Lord my God from the stomach of the fish."

The question naturally arises, If Jonah had reopened the channel of communication with the Lord while drowning in the sea, why did it take so long for him to pray once he was "safe" inside the fish?

The answer may be found in Jonah's stubborn nature. When terror filled his heart with fear, he thought again of the Lord and gave expression to his feelings (cf. Psalm 119:67,71,75). He was repentant; but this did not necessarily mean that he was ready to obey God's will. As the Old Testament counterpart of the prodigal son, he had to be brought to the end of himself. This happened at the end of "the three days and three nights." It was then that he said in effect, "I will arise and go to my Father, and will say to him, 'Father, I have sinned . . .'" (Luke 15:18).

The genuineness of Jonah's experience in the belly of the fish may be gleaned from several specifics in the text. First, there is an emphasis on "his God" in 2:1. This implies complete, personal trust in and a willing submission to His authority. Then, there is the element of repentance seen in the use of *palal,* "prayed," to describe his contact with the Father. *Palal* means "to judge one's self," and when applied to prayer conveys the idea of repeated expressions of contrition. Finally, there is the sincere emotion that permeates his prayer. It does not contain requests but rather breathes the

---

3. The length of Jonah's stay in the fish is described as "three days and three nights." It is used by Christ to parallel His own experience in the grave. Jonah, of course, did not die, but (as with Isaac (see Genesis 22) was positionally dead. The problem arises in the length of time Christ spent in the tomb. If it was a full 72 hours, then the crucifixion could not have taken place on Friday. David Baron, a Hebrew Christian scholar, has the following to say about the Jewish method of calculating time: "According to Jewish law, part of the day stands for the whole.... If a child is born in the last hour or even the last few minutes of a day, it is counted as a whole day of the period of time in which he must be circumcised. Thus *legally*, according to Jewish reckoning, the crucifixion and burial of our Lord having taken place before the 10th Nisan actually commenced, He may be said to have been in the grave 'three days and three nights,' *viz., Friday,* to which legally belonged the night of what we would call Thursday; *Saturday,* consisting of the night of Friday and the day of Saturday; and *Sunday,* to which belonged the night of Saturday and the very early morn of Sunday" (*Types, Psalms and Prophecies* (London: Hodder & Stoughton, 1907), pp. 79-80. Further evidence comes from Sir Robert Anderson's *The Bible and Modern Criticism* (London: Hodder & Stoughton, 1902), p. 272, and J. Lightfoot's *Horae Hebraicae et Talmudicae* (Oxford: University Press, 1859), II:210-11).

atmosphere of thankfulness. In spite of his waywardness, Jonah recognized that God had been gracious to him. Previously, he had been "off center" as far as God's will was concerned. Now he has judged himself and knows God will no longer need to chasten him (cf. 1 Corinthians 11:31).

In the attitude of Jonah we also observe a most important principle of dialogue. Previously he had rationalized his disobedience as being "for the good of his people." Now, however, he was prepared to acknowledge the inappropriateness of what he had done.

Admitting our errors is one of the first steps towards true maturity. If we continue to defend our actions, and feel that we must justify our conduct, we betray our insecurity. When we behave defensively, our friends and associates soon pick up our "signals" and the result is impaired relationships. And where our children are concerned, our poor example models for them a set of negative characteristics. Only by seeing ourselves as God sees us and confessing our shortcomings can we begin to grow in the way He desires. By strengthening our relationship with Him, we can begin to enjoy the security He offers.

When this becomes part of our lives, we radiate confidence to those who are about us. The hesitancy of our peers moves towards a more positive response, and our children feel free to relate to us.

In dealing with our children, we have much to learn from the example God sets for us (cf. Psalm 103:10-11, 14). He was sensitive to Jonah's situation, exercised wisdom and restraint, and yet allowed His prophet to suffer the consequences of his rebellion (Psalms 118:18). At no time did He provoke Jonah with unreasonable demands, teasing or rejection (Ephesians 6:4; Colossians 3:21). Instead, He placed him in an environment where he could reflect on his behavior. In the belly of the fish Jonah finally came to acknowledge his disobedience, and in his prayer he acknowledged God's righteousness and said in effect, "I know I deserve this."

The Cry for Help

We may derive further encouragement from Jonah's prayer. There are numerous occasions in our lives when we "call out to the Lord in our distress" and find that He answers us. No predicament or situation in life ever places us beyond His love and care. God heard Jonah when he was drowning in deep waters and also when he prayed inside the fish. His response was immediate; and He is just as willing to respond to us when we turn to Him in believing faith.

Jeannie was a young Korean girl. At the age of three she lost her sight in the war. Whatever hardships she had faced before were now accentuated. She had to beg for rice to stay alive. Then, when she was five, her father left her on the doorstep of a missionary home for blind orphans. She felt rejected, and for the next five years tried to find meaning and happiness in her dark world.

In time, Jeannie was adopted by a couple in Indiana. After completing some preliminary schooling, she was enrolled in Wheaton Academy, Illinois. Here again disappointment faced her. She found it hard to compete with those who did not share her handicap. During a period of severe depression her American parents came to see her. "You must face the world," her mother told her. "God has helped you come this far, and if you trust Him, He will keep on helping you." With this encouragement, Jeannie persevered. The years were long and the courses hard, but she kept moving forward. Now, as a young woman, she looks back positively on that experience and testifies of the way God worked in her life.

But what made the difference? Two things: acceptance and trust. Jeannie felt loved and wanted by the couple who had adopted her. This gave her a sense of worth. They helped her put her trust in the Lord and, though falteringly at first, she began to draw on Him for help. This gave her hope. As she did so, she developed confidence in herself and a strong inner sense of security.

Jeannie's emotional experience is similar to that of many people today. They are concerned about their acceptance by others and need to feel that they belong. A feeling of acceptance and the security it brings is particularly important in young lives. Continued acceptance by their parents, even when they may have done wrong or appear to be failing to achieve certain goals, is absolutely essential. It helps them develop the "ego strength" they need if they are to persevere when the pressures of life seem to overwhelm them. But coupled with acceptance there should also be a responsive trust--first in their parents and then in the Lord. In childhood and youth they should be encouraged to bring their problems to their parents. This requires that their parents provide the same loving and accepting atmosphere the Lord provides. Then as their sons and daughters grow older, they will find it easy to take the things that concern them to the Lord. This is what Jonah did. He knew that he could call on the Lord and that He would answer him.

All Our Yesterdays

In our progress towards maturity, it is well for us if we can look back on the past and admit that our willful disobedience merited God's disapproval. In this chapter (2:4-7) Jonah readily acknowledged that when all God's "breakers and billows were passing over him" he despaired of life. He felt as if God had rejected him. "I have been expelled from Your sight," he exclaimed. But such was not the case. God was with him in his affliction, tempering every situation in order to sustain his life. Jonah finally came to see the goodness of God. He then addressed the Lord in the most personal of terms: "You have brought up my life from the pit." And with his confidence restored, his basic commitment surfaced once more. He then began to see that his misguided patriotism had blinded his eyes.

Jonah's confidence in the Lord was such that he showed no signs of panic. There was no psychotic break in his experience such as happened in the case of James Bartley. While Jonah did not anticipate deliverance, his faith in God's love and grace was stronger than his fear of death. He now experienced peace, and this peace garrisoned his heart and mind.

A similar situation involving a young mother has recently been brought to our attention. Her husband, Jim, had been in the navy and, even though it was many years since his discharge, he had a dream: He wanted to make a round-the-world trip in a schooner he had recently acquired. His wife, Mary Jane, protested; but in spite of her protests, charts were consulted, a crew was selected and the day of his departure finally dawned. Loving "good-byes" were said, and Mary Jane and the children watched the schooner until it finally disappeared into the haze of the horizon.

Before Jim left, definite plans were made as to the exact day and hour when he would contact Mary Jane by short-wave radio. One day, soon after his departure, the radio call did not come on schedule. Mary Jane waited. The minutes dragged like hours. Her lonely vigil and mounting fears all added to the strain of the situation. "What has happened to him? Where is he? Is he in trouble? How can I reach him?" These and many other questions poured into her mind and brought unrest to her spirit.

Finally, Mary Jane called the Coast Guard. After several days of diligent search, they had nothing to report. "We are very sorry, Mrs. Blackwell," they said. "There is no sign of a boat, wreckage, life raft or survivors of any kind."

At first, Mary Jane's reaction was one of bitter resentment. She hadn't wanted Jim to go on this "foolish" trip. Then depression settled in. Was she still married or a widow? And what of the children? Did they have a father or not? So oppressed did Mary Jane become that it began to affect her life. Despair became her daily companion. Months passed, but her only feelings were ones of pain. The future looked bleak. Life was senseless. She wanted to die. The children suffered, too. Being deprived of a father was bad enough, but in their mother's present state she was of no help to them.

In desperation, Mary Jane decided to visit her pastor. It was many years since she and her husband had been regular attendees at church, but now, in her extremity, she felt that he might be able to help her. In a long session in which she poured out her heart to her pastor, she told him of all her frustrations and fears, bitterness and resentment. She had finally come to the end of herself. It was then that her pastor began encouraging her. "It's no use trying to be a little god and run your own life, Mary," he said. "This will only lead to frustration and emptiness. God loves you. Why not tell

Him what you have told me? He accepts you just as you are. Put your trust in Him and let Him care for you."

Then he waited. Mary Jane spent a long time in thought. Finally, she yielded her life entirely to Jesus Christ. Only then did the peace of God fill her heart, and in the days that followed He lifted her from the depths of despair to a plateau of victory.

After more than two years, Mrs. Blackwell still does not know if she is married or a widow, but the Lord has helped her make the adjustments and concentrate her energies on rearing her children. He has also given her purpose and direction. Life now has meaning. He has taken the core of bitterness and fear from her and replaced it with confidence and trust, enabling her to cope with loneliness and her unanswered questions.

Glimpses of the Inner World

When Jonah "came to himself" and repented of his sin he was led to consider the root cause of his waywardness. As with Mrs. Blackwell, he found that he had set up himself and his system of values as "gods" in his life. "They that regard vain idols (lit., empty vanities)," he confessed, "forsake their own mercy, but I will sacrifice to You with the voice of thanksgiving. That which I have vowed I will pay." In these statements he admitted his culpability; and his self-judgment opened up a new dimension of communication for him.

But what is idolatry? Jonah feared the Lord; how could he be charged with idolatry? His words, however, shed light on the problem for us. Idolatry may be defined as anything that usurps the place of God in our lives (Colossians 3:5). In his case, Jonah had set up the nation, the esteem in which he was held as a patriot, and his own self-will as "rival deities" to the Lord of glory.[4] In a similar way, Christians today may allow ambition (Romans 16:17-18), covetousness (Ephesians 5:5), gluttony (Philippians 3:19), materialism (1 John 2:15-17), loved ones (Luke 14:26), love of praise (John 12:43) or self-will (Luke 9:23) to come between them and the Lord. When they do so, they become guilty of idolatry and, as Jonah pointed out, turn their backs on God, the Source of all mercy (Ephesians 2:4; Titus 3:5). Then, having deprived themselves of His favor, they begin to wonder why their lives are barren and fruitless (cf. Jeremiah 2:13).

The foolishness of such a policy has been described by the writers of the Old Testament.

They show their disdain for idolatry in the contemptuous terms they use to describe it.[5] Through idolatry the glory of God is impugned and mankind is debased; the worshiper becomes like the thing he worships (Hosea 9:10); and, in a very real sense, sorrow and misery follow in the

---

4. Cf. *The Mishnah*, Demai, 6:10; Shabbath 9:6; Sanhedrin 7:4; etc.
5. See Exodus 20:4; Leviticus 19:4; 1 Samuel 31:9; 1 Kings 15:13; Isaiah 44:9-20; 66:3; Jeremiah 20:2-10; 50:38; Ezekiel 16:15-17; 20:31; 23; Hosea 1:2; 8:5; 13:2; etc.

wake of those individuals (and nations) who turn their backs on the Lord.

It is no wonder, therefore, that we all stand indicted on this account. F. Spencer Johnson described his own experience:

> I came to Jesus long ago,
> In love He took me in;
> Alas, I trusted in myself,
> And drifted into sin.
> At last I found the reason why,
> As light came more and more--
> I had a shelf with idols on
> Just behind the door.

And in his famous hymn, "O for a Closer Walk with God," William Cowper encourages us with his example:

> The dearest idol I have known,
> What-e'er that idol be,
> Help me to tear it from Thy throne
> And worship only Thee.

The Way Out

Jonah's repentance was very real. He turned from his sins of willfulness and idolatry to God in confession and made a vow to the Lord.[6] What this vow was we do not know. Sufficient to say that Jonah was happy in the restoration of his relationship with God the Father. He confidently awaited the Lord's "salvation" (Jonah 2:9). The discipline he had received had done its work. His prayer and vow bear eloquent testimony to his submission to the will of God.

What happened next may have come as a surprise to Jonah. "*Yahweh* (the LORD) spoke to the fish and it vomited up Jonah on the dry land." Whether the language is anthropomorphic or not, we have no means of knowing. We do know the result. Jonah was released. Skeptics, however, have discounted the validity of verse ten and have invented all sorts of ingenious ideas--including the dismissal of the whole of chapter two as a later addition to the record--to try to avoid God's active involvement in Jonah's circumstances. But the seemingly miraculous character of the narrative need not surprise us. It is a well-known fact that porpoises and whales beach themselves when they are ill or about to die. Furthermore, as we have already noticed, Frank T. Bullen, in his book *The Cruise of the Cachalot,* has provided us with dramatic eye-witness accounts of sperm whales ejecting from their stomachs lumps of food up to eight feet in diameter. Furthermore, according to *The Boston Post,* Marshall Jenkins was spewed out of the mouth of the whale that had swallowed him, but not before it had sounded to a considerable depth. After being ejected, Jenkins was found to be "much bruised but not seriously hurt."

---

6. *The Mishnah* (Danby's translation), pp. 265-80; also C. J. Barber, *God Has the Answer* ... (Grand Rapids: Baker, 1974), pp. 135-45.

These accounts and others from the early days of whaling, together with more recent scientific observation of whales and their habits, confirm the validity of the biblical record.[7]

One question remains: Where was Jonah when he again set foot on dry land? The Jewish historian, Josephus, claims that this took place on the shores of the Euxine (or Black) Sea. This is most unlikely. The last mention of land is in chapter one, verse thirteen. While the fish could have traveled a considerable distance with Jonah as an unwelcome "passenger," the probability is that Jonah was vomited up somewhere near Joppa, the port from which he had begun his odyssey. He therefore faced a journey of between five to eight weeks (depending upon his physical condition and speed of travel) in order to get to Nineveh. In our next chapter we will consider his journey as well as the result of his ministry in the Assyrian capital.

INTERACTION

1. We, as parents, often find ourselves feeling guilty as we consider the fact that our busyness has kept us from

---

7. For evidence of a man being swallowed by a fish (shark) and later being spewed from its mouth alive, see Edward George Boulenger's *Queer Fish and Other Inhabitants of Rivers and Oceans* (London: Partridge, 1925), pp. 4, 181, 186; Fox's *Sixty-three Years of Engineering*, p. 300; and C. F. Keil, "Jonah," *The Minor Prophets* (Grand Rapids: Eerdmans, n.d.), 1:398n.

spending more time in meaningful interaction with our children. We sense the need to share ourselves, our concerns and our vulnerabilities, as well as our joys and our growth, in an open and honest way. When we do, it provides our children with a visible model to follow. But is it possible that there is a deeper reason for our hesitancy to share ourselves with them? When the popular author, John Powell, shared with his friend the question, "Why am I afraid to tell you who I am?" the friend replied: "Because if I tell you who I am, you might not like who I am and that is all I have." What are the implications of this reply for us as parents? (See 1 John 4:16-21)

2. When God disciplines us (cf. Hebrews 12:5-11), He intends that we learn from our experience. Moses communicated the same concept in Deuteronomy 8:2, 5. What lessons should Jonah have learned following his experiences in the fish? In what ways may these lessons apply to situations we face?

3. How can we design the discipline of our children that it might maximize the opportunity for them to learn from the experience rather than simply change their behavior momentarily to escape possible punishment?

4. From Jonah's experience, we see clearly that part of his prayer was given to self-examination. In light of the fact that God knows our thoughts more completely than we ourselves (see Psalm 139:1-4), what is to be gained

from our self-searching and the resulting confession that is exemplified in Jonah's prayer?

5. Prayer is multifaceted (Jonah 2:2-9) and includes such dimensions as petition; acknowledgment of God's intervention; review of one's own experience, thoughts and feelings; confession; praise and thanksgiving. What pattern have we followed in the past as we have taught our children to pray? How might this be expanded in the future to include these other facets?

NOTES

Chapter 6

FROM INSIGHT TO ACTION

The Bible is filled with practical information on parenthood. The Lord Jesus provides some important insights into the problems of rearing adolescents in His parable of the man who had two sons. Approaching his elder son, the father addressed him in most affectionate terms: "Son, go work today in the vineyard." His words are clear and direct, and demonstrate a reasonable and loving attitude. They are also backed up by the authority vested in him as the head of the household.

To his father's request the son, who was bound to serve on the family estate, replied courteously: "I go, sir." Unfortunately, his ready consent was not followed by appropriate action, and the work remained undone.

The father then sought out his younger son and repeated his request. This son's response was a harsh and discourteous: "I will not." Afterwards, however, this youth experienced a change of heart and obeyed.

"Which one," Christ asks, "did the will of his father?" (Matthew 21:28-31). The answer is obvious: the one who obeyed.

In our study of behavior patterns, we find that there are levels of obedience corresponding to our growth toward maturity. A young child often will respond promptly and cheerfully to a request. He desires to please, and his obedience is almost certain to win him praise. Adolescents, on the other hand, feeling the need to be self-assertive, frequently are unpredictable and may make promises on which they fail to follow through. This results in a lack of a sense of fulfillment that eventually leads to frustration. The ideal is found in those who respond to a request, not out of coercion, but out of love. When this response is God-ward, it is described as "doing the will of God from the heart" (Ephesians 6:6).

The Israelites were God's chosen people (Exodus 19:5). They were to be "a light to the nations"[1] and bring the knowledge of the Lord to those about them. But God's will was neglected and the Jews were content with their position as "favorite sons." They became unwilling to share God's

---

1. See Genesis 17:4-6; 18:18; 22:18; 26:4; Deuteronomy 2:5; 4:6-8; 11:23; 12:2-3; 14:2; 15:6; 26:18-19; 28:1-14; Joshua 2:10-11; etc. In this connection it is important to notice the close association between the "enlarging of Israel's border" and "the place where *Yahweh* your God shall choose *to put His name there...*" in Deuteronomy 12:20-21. Israel failed to fulfill her mission to the nations, and later writers identified the fulfillment of God's intention that all nations be brought under His rule with the inauguration of the Millennial Kingdom (1 Kings 8:41-43; Psalms 67:2-4; 72:11; 86:9-10; 102:15; Isaiah 2:2-4; Jeremiah 16:19; Zephaniah 2:11; Zechariah 14:9, 16).

blessings with others and took pride in their provincialism. In a sense, they may be regarded in the same light as the father's older son who, when asked by the father to "go and work in the vineyard," agreed to do so but failed to follow through on his promise.

Jonah, on the other hand, was similar to the younger son. He at first refused to bring God's message to the Ninevites, but afterwards repented and obeyed. However, as Jonah, chapter 4, confirms, his service was not from the heart. What happened between his release from the belly of the fish and his arrival in Nineveh to bring about his negativitism? Did he view the Ninevites with sibling rivalry? Did he resent the fact that God was taking an interest in them? These questions will be answered as we ponder the personality dynamics involved in this chapter. But first we must consider Jonah's (re) commission.

No Compromise

The way in which God dealt with Jonah is most instructive (Jonah 3). We read, "Now the word of *Yahweh* (the LORD) came to Jonah the second time, saying, 'Arise, go to Nineveh the great city and proclaim against it the proclamation which I will give you.' So Jonah arose and went to Nineveh." Please note that there was no reproach of Jonah for his former disobedience, but only a quiet reiteration of the request. We might have expected an order or a command as when God spoke to the fish (Jonah 2:10), but instead He chose to speak to His servant ("the word of *Yahweh* came to Jonah," 3:1; compare 1:1). To be sure, His word is backed by His authority, but there is no evidence of His displeasure or distrust of Jonah. All He did was ask Jonah to obey Him of his own volition.

When we, as parents, find ourselves in similar situations, particularly following some "power play" (as had until recently characterized Jonah's relationship with God), the tone of our voice or our choice of words may communicate a harsh, distrusting attitude. We may have grown so accustomed to these responses that our attitude and voice level are now "second nature." Our use of them may be designed to reinforce our authority and unwittingly imply that our forgiveness and acceptance of our son or daughter is conditional. What we communicate is, "You've got to prove yourself"--and then we are surprised when our child equates his or her worth as an individual with their ability to please us. But God did not treat Jonah that way! Instead, by His example, He added a new dimension to our understanding of parenthood.

Research has identified three primary patterns of parenting: *authoritarian, authoritative,* and *permissive.*[2]

---

2. For some recent research on the subject, see D. Baumrind, *Genetic Psychology Monograph* LXXV (1967), 43-48; *Adolescence* III, No. 2 (1968), 255-72; and *Developmental Psychology Monographs* IV, No. 1 (1971), 1-103.

The *authoritarian* parent may best be described as attempting to shape, control and evaluate a child's behavior and attitudes according to a set standard of conduct that usually takes the form of absolutes. Obedience is considered a primary virtue, and punitive means are used to curb any expression of self-will. Open communication is not encouraged but rather the child is expected to accept direction without question.

The *permissive* parent is viewed as attempting to behave in a non-punitive, accepting and affirmative manner, and makes few demands on the child. Orderly behavior is expected but not required, and the child is allowed to regulate his or her own activities without control from the parent. Reason is used to attempt changes in behavior and discipline is regarded as degrading to the child.

The *authoritative* parent fits into the middle of these extremes. Active direction is given to the child's activities, but in a manner that is rational and issue-oriented. Open communication is maintained, and reason is given for policies that are established in the home. Both autonomous self-will and disciplined conformity are valued. Firm control is exerted at points of parent-child divergence, but the child is not hemmed in with restrictions. Both the parent's special rights as an adult and the child's individual interests and unique characteristics are recognized. The authoritative parent supports the child's present qualities, freely accepts the child as a person, and is quick to show affection and give praise. Standards are set and expectations are maintained, but without the child coming to feel that his or her worth is dependent upon their performance. Such rearing is designed to give the child adequate security in the home and develop sufficient individual autonomy (or self-assertiveness) in his contact with others.

As we examine the text of Jonah 3, we find that God renews His commission to Jonah in a direct, positive way. His words convey the idea of action. What He says breathes the air of confidence, and yet He is not coercive. If we may borrow the expression used above, He is an authoritative Parent who avoids the extremes of authoritarianism on the one hand and permissiveness on the other. God is also supportive of Jonah. He tells him to go to Nineveh and proclaim the message He will give him. Jonah has previously failed. To allow him to return to Samaria would not be in his best interest, even though it would be the easy (permissive) thing to do. If Jonah does not succeed now, he will live out the rest of his life with the memory of his failure dogging his footsteps. By recommissioning him to go to Nineveh, God reinforces the genuineness of His forgiveness and demonstrates to Jonah the confidence He has in him. Jonah's worth is not related to his performance!

These are important lessons for us to learn. On the one hand, our children need to be assured of our loving involvement, and, on the other hand, they need to demonstrate to themselves that they can succeed. If they do not do so, they may approach adulthood under a cloud of imagined deficiencies.

Blunt Words

Nineveh is approximately five hundred miles from Israel, and it must have taken Jonah approximately six weeks to make the journey. What his thoughts were as he traveled along we do not know. From Jonah chapter 2 we learn that his recent experience has renewed his dedication to the Lord. But his preaching to the people of Nineveh (ch. 3) and his remonstrance with the Lord afterwards (ch. 4) show that on the way to the capital of Assyria, his former jealousy for his people reasserted itself. He is now obedient to the Lord---he has learned his lesson too well to again disobey God--but his obedience seems to be the result of conformity to the will of God rather than from the heart.

Nineveh is described as "the great city." It was, in reality, a "metropolis'" consisting of several cities (Genesis 10:11-12). According to Sir Austen Henry Layard, the first archaeologist to unearth this ancient site, the perimeter around these cities was about 480 stadia (i.e., it had a circumference of approximately 60 miles).[3]

---

3. Layard's observations correspond with those of Didorus Sicilus, II:1-28. See also A. H. Layard, *Nineveh and Babylon* (London: Murray, 1853), p. 640; idem, *Nineveh and Its Remains* (London: Murray, 1851); and George Rawlinson, *Five Great Monarchies of the Ancient Eastern World* (3d ed.; London: Murray, 1871), II:126-27.

As Jonah begins to enter Nineveh and encounters the first group of people, he pauses long enough to utter the barest essentials of the message God has given him. "In forty days Nineveh will be overthrown." Then he passes on. His message is one of impending judgment, but there is no call to repentance nor any mention of the name of the God whom he serves. His preaching is not designed to bring the Ninevites to a place of trust in *Yahweh*, the God of Israel. The usage of the word *haphak*, "to overturn, to overthrow," implies sudden violent destruction.[4] It would instill fear and promote a sense of guilt, but it lacked hope and was devoid of all grace. It also appears as if Jonah went through the capital only and did not extend his ministry to the other cities making up "Greater Nineveh" for there is no record of his ministry lasting for more than one day.

At the Grass Roots

To Jonah's amazement, there is widespread repentance throughout Nineveh. Evidently his message is repeated so that even those who have not seen him in person learn of their plight. Before long, the entire populous is astir. As they consider their conduct in the light of their quickened consciences, they acknowledge the error of their ways. "They believe in God (*'Elohim*), call a fast and put on sackcloth."

---

4. The Niphal participle implies the same kind of holocaust that overtook Sodom and Gomorrah (Genesis 19:21-25, 29).

They show by these actions their sincerity and the genuineness of their repentance.

News of Jonah's message soon reaches the palace. The celebrated historian, Dr. John Kitto, is of the opinion that Jonah was summoned to appear before the king.[5] If this is so, then it explains why the king so quickly rose from his throne, laid aside his robe, covered himself with sackcloth and sat on the ash heap. His example was followed by his nobles. Their sackcloth of camels' or goats' hair was a sign of their grief, and sitting on an ash heap at the city dump was symbolic of their humiliation.

But why these dramatic results? Jonah's preaching did not contain a call to turn from the worship of Nabu (or Nebo) to *Yahweh*, but only a message of doom. In fact, the more closely we study his message, the more serious become its defects.

The answer to this question has plagued expositors and historians for centuries. Its solution is coupled with another question: If Assyria was *the* power in the ancient Near East at this time, why should they fear being overthrown? Several plausible answers have been advanced. First, some Bible expositors feel that the plagues of 765 and 759 B.C.

---

5. See Kitto's *Daily Bible Illustrations* (Edinburgh: Oliphant, 1875), VI:403-04. It is also worth noting that under Adad-nirari, there was an approach to monotheism. This could have aided Jonah's ministry.

and a total eclipse of the sun in 763 B.C. predisposed the people to expect some further catastrophe.[6] This is possible. The weakness of this view lies in the dating of Jonah's ministry. It is probable that his visit to the Assyrian capital took place before these events.

Second, those who place Jonah's ministry earlier in the reign of Jeroboam II point to the internal weakness which plagued the Assyrian empire following the death of Shalmaneser III (859-824 B.C.).[7] Towards the end of his life, his eldest son led a revolt against him. The revolt was suppressed and Shalmaneser's second son ascended his father's throne. However, this son soon died, and Semiramis reigned as regent until Adad-nirari III (810-783 B.C.) was of age. But Adad-nirari was a weak administrator. During this time the people of Urartu (ancient Armenia) assumed independence and became a powerful force north of the Fertile Crescent.[8] Other nations that had been vassals of Assyria refused to pay tribute and stood ready to join with a power-

---

6. Historical evidence for days of national mourning is to be found in the writings of Herodotus (IX:24), Virgil ("Ecologue," V), also *The Aeneid* (XI:80ff.); and Plutarch, ("Alexander," 72). See also T. Laetsch, *Bible Commentary on the Minor Prophets* (St. Louis: Concordia, 1956), pp. 235-36; and D. J. Wiseman, ed., *Peoples of the Old Testament* (Oxford: Clarendon, 1973), p. 160.
7. Jehu, king of Israel, paid tribute to Shalmaneser. Jonah, we have seen, lived during the reign of Jeroboam II. See *Ancient Near Eastern Texts*, p. 281.

ful neighbor in overthrowing a common enemy. As a nation, therefore, Assyria had good cause to fear punitive action.

While these views should not be ignored, most commentators have failed to consider a third possibility. The Lord Jesus stated that, "Jonah became a sign to the Ninevites" (Luke 11:30). At first we are inclined to ask, How? Then, when we remember the description given of James Bartley following his rescue from the stomach of the whale, we come to understand Christ's words in a new light. When James Bartley's skin was exposed to the gastric juices inside the whale, his face, neck and hands were "bleached to a deadly whiteness and took on the appearance of parchment." He also lost all his hair. From this time onwards his skin was particularly sensitive to the sun's rays and never recovered its natural appearance.

We may safely conclude that the same phenomenon happened to Jonah. He became a "sign" of the judgment of God to the Ninevites. They may well have reasoned that if his God would do this to punish the disobedience of one of

---

8. The term "Fertile Crescent" was coined by John Henry Breasted to describe that stretch of land beginning in the Persian Gulf and extending northwest along the Tigris and Euphrates river valley, then continuing west to the Mediterranean before turning south along the Great Rift Valley fault line through Canaan and the Negev. The area embraced by these rivers forms a crescent and is very fertile. The people of Urartu (north of the Fertile Crescent) have been identified with the Hurrians (or Horites) as being Caucasian.

His prophets, what calamities lay in store for them (cf. I Peter 4:17)? And the very presence of Jonah in their city would accentuate their feelings of insecurity. It is no wonder, therefore, that if the king and his nobles saw the disciplining hand of God on Jonah, they quickly issued the following proclamation:

> Do not let man, beast, herd or flock taste anything. Do not let them eat or drink water. Both man and beast must be covered with sackcloth; and let them call on God earnestly; and let each man turn from his wicked way and from the violence which is in his hands. Who knows whether the God[9] may relent and turn away from his burning anger so that we do not perish.

But the repentance of the Ninevites was displeasing to Jonah (4:1). He became very angry when he realized that his strange appearance is furthering their reform, and so he left the city (4:5).

Any other preacher would have been thrilled with even a small percentage of Jonah's success, but Israel's prophet

---

9. The article appears with *'Elohim* indicating that in their repentance the Assyrians turned from the worship of their god to the true God even though they did not know His name. Unfortunately, Jonah's message was so deficient that they were deprived of a knowledge of the uniqueness of Israel's God, *Yahweh*, and this undoubtedly placed limitations on them and reduced the long-term benefits of this unique revival.

was filled with resentment at the thought of God being gracious to another nation. At the basis of Jonah's problem was a distorted view of what God is like. He failed to understand God's grace. Instead of showing the same lovingkindness to those who are outside the "covenants of promise," Jonah acted in a way that demonstrated his personal and spiritual immaturity. *His* "moral rectitude" became the yardstick by which *he* determined whether or not punishment was to be meted out to the Ninevites.

The Problem of Maturity

In terms of our own progress towards maturity, it is well for us to consider the three primary stages of moral development.[10] The first stage is the *preconventional* level at which we are essentially hedonistic and concentrate on satisfying our selfish desires. Others are important to us only insofar as they satisfy our wants. This level of maturity is generally associated with the early years of life. The second stage of development is *conventional* in that we respond to external standards. We take hold of these criteria and make them into absolutes. Our "law and order" mentality is, in reality, an anchor for our insecurity. And, of course, we expect others to abide by the standards that we have adopted. This was the level at which Jonah functioned. Finally, there is the *postconventional* level that functions at

---

10. See Lawrence Kohlberg, *Readings in Values Clarification* (New York: Winston, 1973), pp. 49-61.

a higher standard of righteousness and justice. This is where the difference between law and grace can so readily be seen. There is no lowering of standards or compromise with the truth, but there is an understanding of the limitations of human nature and a reluctance to condemn others. This is the level at which God functions. His justice is balanced by His mercy, and His righteousness is poised with His lovingkindness, and His truth is counterbalanced by His grace. In His dealings with us, we daily experience His love and compassion. Only in the case of persistent, willful rebellion does He move in judgment. This is a prerogative that He reserves for Himself; but it was this very attribute which Jonah assumed. Jonah, unfortunately, operated on a lower level of reasoning and expected God to do likewise.

But before we condemn Jonah for his myopia, let us examine ourselves and consider the example God sets for us as parents. All too often our attitude parallels Jonah's. We are harsh and censorious, instantly ready to inflict a penalty for an offense, call attention to past misdeeds, take out our own frustrations on our children, and produce in them feelings of guilt and fear.

God the Father, however, disciplines us to bring about needed correction and aid our development (Psalm 119:75; Hebrews 12:5-11). He leads and supports us as we face the future and shows His love and concern for us by encouraging us at each stage of our development. This instills in us a deep sense of security and an attitude that is conducive to growth.

The Moral Nexus

On hearing the word of the Lord through Jonah, the Ninevites repent of their sin. They apparently know something of the nature of the One whom they construe as the Supreme Being, for they hope He will be merciful to them. "And when God sees their deeds, how they turn from their wicked way, then God relents concerning the punishment He has declared He will bring upon them, and He does not do it." While God is always displeased with those who transgress His commandments, He is always ready to act in grace toward them when they turn from their sinful way and place their trust in Him.

When we apply these truths to the matter of parenting, it is well for us to be sensitive to changes in the attitude of our children. We should respond to these changes with positive, loving actions and limit our correction of our children to matters of discipline. Only God can act as Judge, for only He knows all the facts and can mete out judgment with justice. This is where Jonah failed. He acted as judge and usurped the place and prerogative of God. As we shall see later on in this book, God did indeed judge the Ninevites, but only after they had spurned His grace.

In our homes, however, we have the responsibility to be authoritative in our role as parents and develop in our children a hearty respect for authority. If our discipline is fair and consistent, then our children will not approach adolescence fearing (and resenting!) "father (or authority) figures" and ready to rebel against all authority. So often, if punishment has taken the place of discipline, resentment against all forms of authority is carried in the hearts of our children. Then, when our sons and daughters leave home, they react against everything their parents have stood for and frequently leave the church as well. If, on the other hand, we take the time to be with our children, are sensitive to their needs, quick to notice changes in their attitudes, and exercise fair and consistent, loving discipline, then we will be able to develop in them a positive regard for authority and aid them in their growth towards maturity.

INTERACTION

1. As we consider the message of Christ's parable (Matthew 21:28-31) in the light of Jonah's own level of obedience, we are challenged to evaluate our own lives. In what areas of our Christian experience may it be somewhat easy for us to willingly acknowledge our Lord's commands but difficult to obey them? How may this problem be overcome?

2. In Matthew 8:5-9 we have the story of a Roman centurion coming to Christ on behalf of his sick servant. He speaks to Christ in terms of the issue of authority, recognizing that he has the authority to give orders to both his servants and the men assigned to his command. God, in his relationship with Jonah, also possesses such

authority and expects His will to be obeyed. Rather than relate to Jonah as a military commander, He communicates with him as to a son, with respect for his personhood and autonomy. In recommissioning Jonah, He simply repeats His request in an authoritative but loving way. How might God's example be applied by us in our directives to our children? Share some examples from your experience where this approach in Jonah 3 has application.

3. Johnny had been asked by his father to carry an important message to the neighbor; but Johnny, for reasons of his own, went off down the street in the opposite direction. His father, at that point, could have more easily carried the message himself, but he took the time to hunt down his son and deal with him regarding his disobedience. He then again directed Johnny to carry out his wishes. Describe what this interaction might have sounded like in keeping with each of the three patterns of parenting described in the chapter.

4. All of us can attest to the painful effects of failure we have experienced in our own lives: feelings of guilt, loss of confidence and fear of criticism and/or humiliation. We see in God's dealings with Jonah (3:1) His purposeful avoidance of criticism and complete absence of any reminder to Jonah of his failure and disobedience. How might we apply this to our own situation? Are

there other ways as well by which we might encourage our children to overcome their failures?

5. As we consider the issue of moral development and maturity, we see our goal as parents as that of helping our children develop an internalized set of values. The ideal was stated by Christ in Matthew 22:37-40. Therefore, instead of saying to our children, "Do this because I say so," or "because our church expects it of us," we should say, "Let's look at what God has to say about this and try to understand why He would want us to do it." Such an approach will have the effect of helping our sons and daughters to develop a rationale for the values we live by. What are some of the areas in which you might begin to work along these lines with your own children?

NOTES

Chapter 7

A PRICKLY PROFILE

During a series of special lectures at the Rosemead Graduate School of Psychology, California, the faculty and students were shown a film. It concerned a young boy named Tommy, who was experiencing great difficulty relating to the children in his neighborhood. He was continually getting into scrapes and always losing.

Tommy's parents became so concerned that they enlisted the aid of a Christian psychologist. Before any action was taken, it was decided to make a film of Tommy's behavior. This film would include his conduct both in the classroom and on the playground. It was hoped that in this way an exact record of all the factors contributing to Tommy's problem could be established.

During the time the film was being made, the psychologist and his staff noticed a pattern of behavior that included both provocation by Tommy and hostility on the part of his "friends." It was also noted on one occasion that Tommy's peers (free from adult supervision) attacked Tommy without provocation and pounded him unmercifully. On another occasion, when Tommy and his "friends" were playing together in a room, his "friends" not only sought an occasion to begin their aggressive behavior but kicked and trampled

Tommy and only stopped when he was weeping and completely beaten in spirit.[1]

The climax to the preliminary research came when the mothers of Tommy's peers were shown the film. They completely bypassed their own sons' behavior and readily picked out those instances where Tommy was obviously the aggressor. In probing the cause of Tommy's problem, the psychologist uncovered the fact that the mothers of Tommy's classmates were so blinded by love and loyalty to their own children that they lacked objectivity. They could not see the errors in their own sons' behavior and were subconsciously blocking their awareness of the truth. The result was the projection of all the blame on Tommy.[2]

In a very real sense, Jonah's behavior parallels this, for he was so concerned over Israel and so anxious to maintain his country's "favored son" status that he overlooked their spiritual waywardness and saw only the evil of Nineveh.

---

1. It should be noted that this particular incident took place in a specially designed playroom with the psychologist and his camera crew in another room. Furthermore, the psychologist interrupted the children at "play" no less that four times to intervene on Tommy's behalf.
2. When the fathers of Tommy's peers were shown the film, they manifested clearer objectivity and readily noticed their sons' misbehavior. This is the way it is with God the Father. He notices our actions and can take appropriate action to correct our attitude and conduct. Jonah was too emotionally involved with His own people to be objective.

Does this seem strange? It shouldn't. Jonah was human and he shared the same concerns as the mothers just mentioned. But how could he, a prophet of the Lord, be guilty of such blindness? How could he overlook the culpability of his people and manifest such an unforgiving spirit?

The answer seems to lie in the vital connection between doctrine and experience, between precept and practice. As with us, Jonah tended to emphasize only those truths that were pleasing to him. And we, as with Jonah, all too often tend to emphasize God's love and forget His righteousness, or we dwell on His justice (particularly where the sin of others is concerned) and overlook His mercy. This is what Jonah did, and in doing so he shows his kinship with us.

About Our Emotions

This chapter is filled with emotional overtones, and the more we probe Jonah's responses, the clearer becomes our picture of the inner working of his heart. The text records: "But [the repentance of the Ninevites] greatly displeased Jonah, and he became angry [lit., hot]."[3] Jonah should have

---

3. The Hebrew *charah*, "to burn, to be kindled" (Jonah 4:1) is always used of anger (Genesis 31:36; 34:7; 1 Samuel 15:11, etc.), and may be accompanied by a visible kindling of anger in the eyes or the inflaming of the countenance (Genesis 31:35; 45:5). *Charah* differs from *aph* (Jonah 4:2) which connotes the idea of hard breathing (Proverbs 22:24; 29:22; see also Deuteronomy 29:19; 32:22; Job 36:13).

been thankful. God had recently shown him mercy by sparing his life. He had also exhibited His grace by recommissioning him. And then crowned his ministry to the Ninevites with success. Jonah could have been a powerful witness of the love and grace of God. Instead, we hear only his bitter remonstrance: "Wasn't this exactly what I said would happen while I was still in my own country?"[4]

Now anger is generally triggered by one or more of three things: (1) The *humiliation* we feel when people look down on us or belittle us; (2) Our experience of *rejection* when we want a relationship with someone and they refuse us; and (3) Our feeling of *frustration* when our plans go awry and we sense that we are no longer in control of the circumstances that surround us. These three reactions rob us of a healthy sense of esteem, deprive us of our feelings of belonging, and undermine our confidence. In his anger, Jonah reveals the petty, narrow, bigoted spirit of his nation. They were the people of the Lord. His blessings were their special possession--or so they thought. Nineveh, on the other hand, was their enemy. The Israelites would rather see them destroyed than contribute toward their repentance. They could not tolerate the idea of Gentiles sharing in what they believed to be their exclusive right.

---

4. The truth of Jonah 3:10 did not become apparent until 40 days had expired. In Jonah chap. 4, the prophet surmised that God would be gracious to them. He nevertheless waited outside the city in the hope that their repentance would wear off and the people of Urartu (Armenia) overrun them.

But how does all of this apply to us? Our emotions either build up or tear down our relationships. Love is the primary constructive emotion. That is why the Lord Jesus said, "A new commandment I give to you that you love one another even as I have loved you . . . By this shall all men know that you are My disciples" (John 13:34-35; see also 15:12,17). *Hostility, guilt* and *fear* are destructive relational emotions that ruin our interpersonal relationships. Jonah, according to verse one, is an example of emotional hostility. He wanted God to move in and judge the Ninevites, and he became angry when he thought that God might not. When we react in this way, a tension develops between our need for inner peace and the way we feel. This serves to aggravate the situation. As with Jonah, we may be too sensitive to be able to live with such burning anger inside us. We, therefore, do what he did and project our anger outward onto someone else. In Jonah's case, there was no one he could blame except God. With wounded pride he chided the Lord by saying in effect, "Wasn't this what I said would happen while I was still in my own land?[5] I wanted to avoid this kind of unpleasant confrontation, and that is why I decided to go to Tarshish."

---

5. Rabbi Cohen affirms that these words do not mean that Jonah spoke to God–there is no record of such communication in chapter 1. They do, however, represent Jonah's thoughts (which were open to the Lord) and the reason for his flight to Tarshish. See *The Twelve Prophets* (London: Soncino Press, 1961), p. 148.

All too often we act as Jonah did. However plausible our reasoning may be, the projection of blame onto another fails to ease the hurt we feel. We crave the peace that only love and acceptance can bring. We may pray, even as Jonah prayed, but, unless our prayer is coupled with confession, it demonstrates only our desire to experience again the heart's ease we have lost. Our need is to be reconciled to God (and those we may have wronged) through confession and forgiveness before we can again experience peace (cf. Matthew 6:12, 14-15; Luke 6:27-49). Only then will we experience again the joy of the Lord. But let us look more intently at Jonah's prayer, for there is a great deal we can learn from it that will explain the way we sometimes think and feel.

Shaft of Light

Jonah's prayer reveals his inner anguish. He is emotionally confused and upset. The words of his prayer are, in reality, a cry for help. In addressing the Lord, he is mindful of the covenant relationship that exists between them. However, he is also acting like a child who feels his world is coming apart at the seams. He is angry with himself for not succeeding with his plan. And he is angry with God for not making things work the way he wanted. Regardless of the words he uses to show his resentment, he is attempting to cover his hurt feelings.

Sometimes in our experience as parents, we encounter the same kind of conduct in our children. A wise mother or father will not commiserate with a child that is feeling hurt or angry, or blame his friends for the circumstances he faces. To do so will only encourage an unhealthy sense of self-pity and deprive him or her of a lesson he or she needs to learn. Instead, a parent should do what God the Father did with Jonah--be ready to listen and in this way provide the child with the security and understanding he or she needs. Such an approach will help the child work his way through the problem.

In examining Jonah's prayer, we find that his knowledge of God is far more praiseworthy than his conduct. He knows the fallacy of doing evil in the hope that good may come from his actions (cf. Romans 6:1-2), but this does not deter him from trying. In the end, however, having proved the futility of his efforts, he admits: "I know that You are a gracious and compassionate God, slow to anger and abundant in lovingkindness and One who relents [where there is repentance] of evil."

In recounting God's attributes, Jonah teaches us that the Lord warns people of judgment so that He may spare them, and admonishes them in order that He might save them. He is merciful, slow to anger, and always ready to demonstrate His lovingkindness to those who turn to Him in faith.

These attributes of grace and compassion, patience and love, are illustrated for us in the example of the Lord Jesus Christ. It was said of Him that He was "full of grace and truth" (John 1:17). This is a most notable statement. So often, in our practice of these virtues, we veer off to one extreme or the other. We either are so gracious that we compromise the truth, or we stand so tenaciously for the truth that we manifest little, if any, grace.

Reason and Responsibility

On one occasion the Lord Jesus was tested by the religious hierarchy of His day. They brought to Him a woman who had been seized in the act of adultery (John 8:1-11). The perfect tense of the verb points to her continuing character as an adulteress, and this probably made it easy for the scribes and Pharisees to set a trap for her.[6] She was thrust before the Lord Jesus with the demand that He pronounce sentence upon her.

The Master, we know, was able to silence her accusers by saying, "Let him who is without sin among you be the first to throw a stone at her." But how did He handle the woman? He first asked, "Where are your accusers?" (a legal necessity if judgment was to be pronounced). When He found that there were none, He said to her, "Neither do I condemn you [grace]; go your way [mercy in the form of a

---

6. Jewish law required that the witnesses see the couple *in coitu*, in the very act. The woman's loose morals made it easy for the scribes and Pharisees to set a trap for her. But where was the man who had engaged in sexual relations with her? (cf. Leviticus 20:10; Deuteronomy 22:22). The law required that *both* be tried and, if found guilty, *both* be sentenced to death.

new opportunity]; from now on sin no more [truth coupled with responsibility]." In this we see His perfect blending of grace and truth. At no time did He condone her sin. Instead, He showed His mercy by giving her the opportunity to repent, experience forgiveness, and make a new life for herself.

In the way the Lord Jesus handled this delicate situation, He neither compromised the truth nor weakened the effect of grace. Both qualities were perfectly balanced in His person. And the same attitude characterized God's dealings with Nineveh. But Jonah, as with the scribes and Pharisees of Christ's day, would have preferred to hear a different verdict.

The Past Is Present

Before we continue with our study of Jonah's prayer, let us pause for a moment to analyze the principles of effective parenting which God's attributes illustrate for us. It is difficult for us, as parents, to model ourselves after a perfect heavenly Father; and yet, what better example could we have? To be sure, we will fail; but by recognizing our need for growth and by relying upon the enabling ministry of the Holy Spirit, we will be able increasingly to follow His example.

Graciousness is basic to godly parenting. A gracious parent is responsive to the needs of his or her children. But grace does not imply overindulgence. Being gracious does not mean that we constantly defer to our children. It does mean that we consistently strive to demonstrate a loving and kind attitude, and that we are always ready to encourage our sons and daughters, quick to forgive, and constant in our nurture of them. This can best be achieved by providing a climate of confidence and seasoned discretion.

Compassion will also play a large part in fostering the proper development of our children. This does not involve doing everything for them or protecting them from stressful situations. To do so would be to rob them of many valuable experiences. True compassion necessitates that we provide them with a "shoulder to cry on" when the going is rough--even as Jonah in his prayer was able to unburden himself to the Lord--and encourage them to pick up the pieces of their shattered world and try again. This will require genuine loving involvement with them in what they are doing and the kind of understanding that communicates our unconditional acceptance of them.

And then there is *patience:* being "slow to anger." So often our own emotions become frayed, and, when something else goes wrong, we react impatiently or even angrily to a relatively minor problem.

But there are other occasions when we may be "slow to anger" because we are afraid to deal with the problem or are so taken up with our own concerns that we do not want to be bothered with Johnny's cut finger or the stain on Mary's dress. Such actions cannot be likened to God the Father's attitude. Throughout the story we see His involvement with Jonah, even when Jonah's actions required that He discipline him. In His discipline of Jonah, He is seen to be "slow to anger."

Graciousness, compassion, patience--these are the characteristics we must develop as we model ourselves after God's example. He is not over-indulgent, but in His abounding love and kindness He gives us more than enough. And let us not overlook the fact that we, at best, may give our sons and daughters just enough time and attention to satisfy them. Then, as soon as they appear satisfied, we take up our pursuits again. Frequently, however, we treat their interruptions as an annoyance and are quick to tell them to "go outside and play." God's loving involvement with us, however, runs over. It is abundant. There is an ample sufficiency for our every need. It is always available for us to appropriate. His kindness extends to the loving discipline of those who are His and, as soon as this has achieved its purpose and a repentant attitude is manifested, He immediately forgives. There is no harboring of grudges or placing us on probation. He recognizes our frailty (even as He did Jonah's) and is willing to work with us and our limitations. His positive actions produce positive results; and His example serves as our guide in the parenting process.

Irrational Desire

While God had been actively involved in Jonah's life in the past few weeks, Jonah's frustration had blinded his eyes to the real issues. Now, in a spirit of acute disappointment, he prays, "Therefore now, O *Yahweh*, please take my life from me, for death is better to me than life."

These words of Jonah's give us another look at our emotional natures. Anger is irrational and self-justifying. The angry person is always right in his or her own eyes. As Jonah perceived his situation, he had failed to stop the repentance of the Ninevites. He became frustrated. He believed that his motives and his cause were right. At first, he projected his hostility outward onto God, but this caused conflict with his beliefs about God. He knew better than to blame God for his failure. Jonah's anger then turned inward on himself. He felt the pangs of guilt because his heart was cold toward God. The Ninevites were responding to God's love and grace, and he was not. All of this served to increase his feelings of hopelessness and intensify his feelings of worthlessness.

Guilt is self-destructive. Those who find that they cannot ease their feelings of unworthiness invariably find some way to punish themselves. Here's how: Instead of availing themselves of the provision God has made for their restoration to His favor, they feel that by denying themselves the blessings He has offered them, they can atone for their sin. The entire cycle is self-defeating. In the case of Jonah, his anger turned inward. His outlook was dominated entirely by his perception of the situation. It appeared hopeless. He had failed. It is no wonder, therefore, that he prayed for death.

There is another factor, however, which frequently prevents people from enjoying the fruits of their Christian experience. It is fear--fear that submission to the Lord will result in changes in their life style. In a sense, Jonah's attitude toward his people (i.e., his patriotism) constituted his security. Submission to the will of God would require a change in his outlook. This made him feel insecure. For Jonah to progress toward personal maturity he must, of necessity, re-evaluate his system of values. He must broaden his outlook of God and His ways with mankind. When he did so, he realized that even Israel was responsible for its actions and must account to God for its sins. He also found that his trust in the Lord replaced his fear of change. But such a change was still future. So far, all he had succeeded in doing was placing God in a position inferior to his nation's interests, and this had resulted in multiplying his trials, adding to his troubles, and causing him unnecessary inner turmoil.

Infinite Patience

It is significant that God did not reprove Jonah or cast him off. He continued to treat him as a son. In responding to Jonah's immaturity, God avoided dealing with surface issues. He passed by the prophet's request for death and went instead to the heart of the matter. "Do you have good reason to be angry?" In other words, "What is the source of your anger, Jonah?" In failing to grant Jonah's request, God also showed him the same grace and compassion He had shown the Ninevites (and magnanimously gave Jonah the very thing he would have denied the Assyrians).

God's question caused Jonah to think. He could not respond to God's words solely on the basis of his emotions. He had to put his mind in gear. Only with his intellect and his sensibilities working together could his will respond appropriately.

But according to the text, Jonah did not respond to the Lord's question. Instead, he climbed to the top of a hill where he could watch what was taking place in the valley below. His actions seem to indicate the same intransigence that had blocked communication at the first. God, however, neither rebuked His servant nor demanded of him an answer. He was patient. As a wise "Parent" he had respect for Jonah's personhood. His question would, in time, lead Jonah to resolve his problem and learn from the experience.

In this respect, God the Father sets a further example for us. We often require some verbal compliance from our children without allowing the normal thought processes to run their course. All we succeed in obtaining from them is the kind of answer they have learned we want to hear. Our insistence on some form of response prevents the ideas we wish to communicate from filtering through their mental processes. God, however, was interested in Jonah's maturity, not his conformity; and, as we shall see in our next chapter, He continued to work behind the scenes to bring about growth in Jonah's personality.

INTERACTION

As a means of interacting with the ideas presented concerning Jonah's emotional response to anger his method of handling his feelings and God's response, consider the following incident:

Four families, anticipating much fun and fellowship, were spending the weekend at a lake. Following lunch, the men carried the cold chests and picnic supplies back to the vehicles, leaving the wives sunning themselves and talking on the beach. The men then wandered toward the dock pondering their next activity. On impulse, they decided to take the children who were with them out on a boat--but they failed to inform their wives, who remained on the beach.

About 45 minutes later, the men headed the boat back to the dock. As they approached, they saw the women waiting for them. It didn't require a great abundance of sensitivity to recognize that their wives were feeling abandoned, ignored, and not too important to their husbands.

Hurt and anger were the emotions of the moment. As the husbands alighted from the boat, the wives responded to their husbands in terms of their feelings and how they were handling them.

At this point, it is important to note that there are four basic methods of handling our feelings of hurt and anger, each with its own typical response in the other person and resulting consequence in our relationship. The chart on the following page sets forth these four methods.

Using the situation described (or creating your own from personal experience), select individuals from your group to role-play each of the four methods explained in this chart. Following the role-play, discuss the effect each of these encounters would have on the children. What would be their feelings? How might they respond? What would they be learning as a result?

ANGER AND THE WAYS WE HANDLE IT

EXTREME OF REPRESSION	SUBCONSCIOUS REPRESSION (Involuntary Total Denial of Anger)	CONSCIOUS SUPPRESSION (Deliberate withholding of Anger)	CONTROLLED CONFESSION. (*Reasoned Owning and Communication of anger.*) **THIS IS THE IDEAL**	EXPRESSION (Destructive "Dumping" of Anger)
TENSION	ANGER RETAINED		ANGER RELEASED	
Provoking Incident — Internal Response	Denial of anger. Projection of "sweet, tolerant" image. Rationalization of provoking incident.	Awareness of anger. Fear of expression. May feel rising resentment.	Awareness of anger and its source. Acceptance of personal responsibility for the anger. Willing to risk confrontation.	Incident perceived as a personal affront. Anger builds and blame is projected on to the other person.
SELF — External Response	*"That's alright, Honey. I know you need to be with others."*	(Says little or nothing. Gives him, the "silent treatment.") Or, *"You know why I'm angry"* – but withholds information.	*"Honey, I'm angry. I really feel rejected."*	*"@#$%&!!"* (Some strong expression of pent-up emotion of an accusing or punishing nature.
OTHER — Internal Response	Self-justification. I have a right to go off with others.	He senses her displeasure. (Questions source. May not be aware of cause.) May ask what is wrong or try to make amends. May either excuse his behavior or blame himself.	Accepts the other person's feelings as genuine and valid for them. Is willing to explore the source of the conflict. Acknowledges his part in provoking incident. *"I can see why you are upset. I am sorry for my thoughtlessness (or insensitivity). How can we set things right?"*	Response perceived as a personal attack. Inner feeling of fear or insecurity is expressed in self-defense. Result: Reciprocal anger and tendency to counterattack.
OTHER — External Reception	*"Why thank you, Honey, for being so understanding."*	*"Let me explain…"* or *"Let me make it up to you."* Continuous "cold war," alternating with "uneasy truces."		*"Why don't you get off my back? You're always nagging me about something."*
Consequence to the Repression	Continued projected image of understanding leading to a false sense of well-being		Growth in mutual understanding. Awareness that conflicts can be solved and the relationship strengthened.	Alienation. Withdrawal to nurse hurt feelings. Tendency to turn to others for nurturance.

NOTES

Chapter 8

A MATTER OF TIME

There are many Bible teachers who, as they conclude their treatment of this small book, believe with John Calvin that Jonah had more respect for his own reputation as a prophet than he had either for the good of Nineveh or the glory of God. They look at the anger he demonstrated in the closing scene, his seeming inability to respond to God's love, the way in which he appears to be locked into an adolescent style of thinking, and they conclude that God could do nothing with him.

Others carry this view a step further. They claim that, though Jonah could do nothing to hinder the divine will, he "secretly deplored the sparing of Nineveh all the days of his life." They also believe that he returned to his own land a bitter, disillusioned man, where, under the hand of the Spirit of God, but still resisting the divine will, he felt compelled to write his memoirs. After this, history graciously "wrapped his ministry in the deepest obscurity." According to these writers, his lasting contribution was his revelation to his fellow-countrymen of the true nature and compassion of God--something which he himself was unable to comprehend.

Let it be said that if Jonah had done nothing other than write this book, the glimpse he gives us of the heart of God the Father[1] would be sufficient to instruct us. But is this all? Did Jonah steadfastly refuse to recognize the love of God to the end of his days? When writing to the Christians at Philippi, Paul said "Of this I am certain: The One who began a good work in you will bring it to completion." (Philippians 1:6). God's work in Jonah's heart did not cease with the end of this book. We have read of His dealings with Jonah, but the termination of the narrative does not imply that His work in Jonah came to a grinding halt.

Out of Focus

But let us return to our story. In our last chapter we left Jonah sitting on a hill overlooking Nineveh. His perception of the repentance of the Ninevites was colored by his national bigotry. He hoped, of course, that the repentance of those in Nineveh would be short-lived and that God still would punish them.

In this respect, Jonah's feelings often parallel our own. Let a child in the neighborhood threaten one of our children (as Nineveh constituted a threat to Israel) and our anger is aroused. And even if there is an expression of regret on the part of the would-be aggressor and assurance that the inci-

---

1. When asked to define love, Dr. Erich Fromm replied, "The most beautiful definition I know of is to be found in the New Testament. Another beautiful definition is the one you will find in the Old Testament in the Book of Jonah. " (See his People in Your Life (Freeport, NY: Books for Libraries, 1971), p. 25).

dent will not be repeated, we still adopt a "wait and see" attitude. Those who have offended us are, in a very real sense, on probation.

Equally as tragic is this attitude when applied to our own sons and daughters. One slip, even a minor one, and we may pounce on them. When they acknowledge their error, it is to find that true forgiveness may be long in coming. They feel as if they are continuously being tested. This undermines their sense of being trustworthy and acceptable, and distorts their view of God--for they begin to think of Him in terms of how they see us relating to them. And this confuses in their minds the distinction between discipline and punishment.

If God really was through with Jonah, then it would have been easy to bring down the curtain on the narrative with the prophet sitting disconsolately on a hill outside the city. But God had not concluded His dealings with His prophet. Whereas previously He had disciplined him, now He will nurture him.

Total Amnesty

From Jonah's vantage point overlooking the water courses, gates, walls and palaces of Nineveh, he can hear the mournful lowing of the cattle and the plaintive bleating of the sheep (Jonah 4:5). He can also see the people going about in sackcloth and their king sitting on top of the city dump. As he looks down on this spectacle of national mourning, hope for the overthrow of Nineveh grows exceedingly faint. And with the fading of his plans, anger (arising from the frustration of his desires and aggravated by his general discomfort) begins to well up inside him.

God, however, knows the inner workings of Jonah's heart. He sees that he is hostile and depressed. Communication is out of the question. Jonah is too angry for Him to speak with him right now. How then can God the Father deal with him? The text affirms that "the LORD (Yahweh) God appointed a plant and it grew up over Jonah to be a shade over his head to deliver him from his discomfort" (Jonah 4:6).

Two questions arise from this statement, and the answers we give them will reveal more of the ways in which God the Father deals with His children: First, what relevance is there in the usage of the combined names Yahweh Elohim; and, second, what does God hope to gain by causing a plant to grow?

Yahweh, "LORD," as we have seen, is the name that links God inseparably with the national awareness and covenant blessings of Israel. It is obviously the term with which Jonah would be most familiar and the one which would bring him the most comfort. 'Elohim, "God," was the term widely used among the Gentiles. It designated power and might. When combined, these two names for God emphasize His love and grace on the one hand, and His superiority as the Creator over His creatures on the other. We are not

His equal. Our awareness of who God is should elicit from us loving submission and loyal service. But Jonah fails to realize the true nature of the One who is even now furthering his spiritual development.

The plant which God caused to grow up so quickly was probably a castor oil plant (ricinus communis) or Palmchrist.[2] It grows rapidly and attains a height of between eight to ten feet. It has broad leaves like those of a vine and these provide welcome shelter from the sun's rays. In Jonah's experience, the usual rapid rate of growth of this plant was accelerated. When he awakened the next morning, it already covered his booth where the leaves on the branches of the trees he had cut down the day before were beginning to wither.

"But what," may we ask, "was Jonah's response to the goodness of God? Was there any recognition on his part of divine intervention (namely, the sudden appearance of the plant) in exactly the right place and at exactly the right time to meet his need? And was there any expression of thankfulness to the Lord for His gracious provision?"

No! Jonah accepted what has happened as if it were his inalienable right. His heart is not softened by this obvious

---

2. The "castor oil plant" or Palmchrist attracted the attention of writers of antiquity, and their descriptions are most interesting, see Pliny, 15:7 and Herodotus II:94.

token of God's awareness of his condition, and there was no response of gratitude to the Lord for easing his suffering.

But what had God hoped to achieve by causing the plant to grow?

Apparently God aimed at penetrating Jonah's defenses by ministering to his primary need. He did what many a mother or father has done under similar circumstances: fix a broken bicycle; shower silent, loving attention on one whose disobedience has resulted in some injury; or prepare a favorite meal . . . and all with a view to opening the channel of communication once more. A gift might pacify, but its significance would be short lived, whereas a loving act is far more likely to elicit a positive response.

God knew of the sensitivity of Jonah's skin to the sun's rays and caused the plant to grow to deliver Jonah from his discomfort. The kind of strategy He employed is preferable to that practiced by some parents who, when a clash of wills occurs, attempt to instill guilt in their child, and may respond by saying, "But look at all I've done for you. Can't you even do this small thing for me?" Or, "It really hurts me to see you behave this way. All I ask is --- ." By comparison, God's approach to the stubborn rebellion of Jonah is infinitely superior. His kindness, not in lavishing Jonah with gifts, but in ministering to a felt need is designed to bring Jonah to experience the warming influence of His love (cf. Matthew 5:44).

Ill-Tempered Response

Unfortunately, while Jonah was in touch with his physical needs, he was totally out of touch with his deeper emotional problems. He was glad for the plant, but took for granted its appearance and remarkable growth and never paused to thank God for His love and grace.

Thankfulness is a recognition and valuing of another person. It involves opening up one's heart and expressing appreciation for the other person's thoughtfulness and concern for us. Had Jonah been thankful, God could have stepped in with encouragement that would have reinforced the step Jonah had taken. Such encouragement could have tended to elicit further communication and movement toward understanding of his Father's love. And this Jonah did not want. He preferred to nurse his anger to keep it warm.

Jonah's thanklessness indicates that his heart is still closed to God. His attitude demonstrates clearly that, at the present time, he is oriented only towards externals and he demonstrates little (if any) spiritual sensitivity. He, therefore, stubbornly refuses to open his heart to the Lord.

God, however, desires to produce empathy in Jonah. He has not been caught unawares by Jonah's recalcitrance and is prepared for the next step. This takes the form of a black caterpillar -something very common in the Near East-that He sends to gnaw away at the bark and stem of the plant

(Jonah 4:7-8). When Jonah awakens the next morning it is to find that the plant is beginning to die. This discovery evokes pity (an emotional response) for the early demise of something he had come to appreciate for its beauty and comfort. And so what God was unable to do by being kind to Jonah He achieves with the death of the plant.

But some may be inclined to ask, "Hasn't God become 'an Indian giver'? How can He, as a Parent, justify giving one of His children something one day, only to take it from him the next?"

It should be pointed out that God graciously gave Jonah something he did not deserve. Jonah had not worked for the plant or contributed to its growth. In causing the worm to eat around the stem of the plant, God was furthering His work in Jonah's heart. The process of bringing Jonah to maturity was more important than a plant which Jonah would have been forced to leave behind him when he returned to his homeland.

We should also observe that God is in sovereign control of the situation. He appointed the objects of His creation to do His will. In His actions there was no "overkill." His planning was long range. His ultimate goal was Jonah's emotional and spiritual growth, not the bestowal of temporal gifts.

When we, as parents, attempt to follow the example of God the Father, we will immediately find that we must think through the issues and plan ahead. We will also find that we must aim at change from within, not conformity from without. This will necessitate that we be responsive to our sons and daughters all the time, not solely in times of crisis.

The Crucial Test

Jonah, however, is now even more unwilling to talk to God. He feels sorry for the plant, but anger continues to choke the channels of communication. God, in His wisdom, now allows Jonah to experience the discomfort brought on by his initial disobedience-the same discomfort he would have had to endure had the plant never grown up to cast its shade on him. This happens as the sun begins to beat down through the withered leaves of the booth.

Then, God appoints a scorching sirocco to blow across the valley (cf. Ezekiel 16:10).[3] Of course, those in Nineveh who are in sackcloth must endure the same unbearable heat; but Jonah, having elected to leave the city, is exposed to the driving sand as well. He is poorly protected, and his skin is unduly sensitive to these discomforts. As the temperature rises, he becomes faint and again prays that he might die.

In dealing with Jonah in this way, God has given us an example of aversive discipline. Jonah is made extremely

---

3. See W. M. Thomson, *The Land and the Book* (Grand Rapids: Baker, 1966), pp. 536-37.

uncomfortable but his well being is in no way threatened. God knows that Jonah will survive. As soon as the hot wind passes, cool refreshing breezes will replace it. For now, however, He is disciplining Jonah in keeping with his stubbornness and resistance to His will.

In requesting to be allowed to die, Jonah shows once more his retrogression to adolescent rebellion. A teenager, as soon as he does not succeed with his plan or cannot get his way, says in effect, "I quit." And those who work with youth in our churches and on committees know how prevalent this attitude is. Adolescents have only a short term ability to cope with adversity. They want autonomy, but show themselves limited in their ability to shoulder adequate responsibility. The predicaments in which they find themselves are frequently a direct result of their behavior; they are not being able to cope with their limitations in a mature way, they resign from their responsibilities.

The Key Issue

When Jonah opens the channels of communication by asking God to allow him to die, the Lord has the opportunity to penetrate his defenses, "Do you have good reason to be angry about the plant?" He asks.[4] Jonah's uncomfortable surroundings have lessened his resistance. His response to God's inquiry is to explode. All his pent up frustration, resentment and the bitterness generated by the past few weeks, gushes out. "I have good reason to be angry," he storms, "even unto death." His mind and emotions are now working together. God's question has called for a rational explanation of his anger. To answer Him, Jonah must think through the issues. This is a process he has so far refused to do.

Jonah, of course, has been slow to learn the lesson God has taken such pains to teach him. And sometimes when we, as parents, become discouraged, we can remind ourselves of the way God dealt with His prophet. Of great help to us will be the development of the ability to ask good questions.[5] Notice how the Lord phrases His question to Jonah. "Do you have good reason [a mental rationale] to be angry [an emotional condition]?" He did not say, "Why do you pity the plant when you have no pity for the people of Nineveh?" Such a question would have placed Jonah on the defensive. Instead, God's question centers on Jonah's motive which ties directly into his emotions.

With the pressure of Jonah's suppressed anger and resentment released, God continues speaking to him. He

---

4. This is the same question as in 4:4, only now with the addition of the words "for the plant." God's question elicits a negative reply from Jonah. God, however, does not condemn Jonah, but allows his own words (and anger) to convince him of the error of his ways.
5. See "The Psychology of Good Questions," in *Dynamics of Effective Leadership: Learning From Nehemiah* (Ross-shire, Scotland: Christian Focus, 2004), pp. 34-36

verbalizes Jonah's feelings and tactfully shows him that He is aware of how he feels. "You had compassion on the plant," the Lord affirms, "and shouldn't I have compassion on Nineveh . . . in which there are more than 120,000 children who have not yet come to years of discernment, not to mention many animals?"

In dealing with Jonah, God the Father gave him important insights into His own nature. He was gracious and showed that He is ready to extend His mercy to those who turn to Him in faith. He is also involved with His creatures and has compassion on those who are young and would perish needlessly if Nineveh were overthrown. His actions reveal that His loving concern extends to all parts of His creation.

Post Script

How long Jonah continued to sit on the hill outside the city cannot be determined with certainty. Of one thing we may be sure: When he returned to Israel his fellow countrymen were able to see in his body the signs of God's judgment. This added weight to the message he communicated to them.

Jonah lived at least to the time of Joel, and probably taught him in the "School of the Prophets." His ministry to Israel was enriched in a two fold way as a result of his experiences. He now knew the sinfulness of Israel's narrow, religious provincialism, and he saw clearly the love and compassion of God toward the lost.

But why does the book end the way it does? Perhaps to show us, as parents, that growth toward maturity takes time. We will not always be able to observe the results of our training in the lives of our children. There will come a time when they will "leave the nest" and we will no longer be able to watch over their development as we did formerly. When this happens, we can take comfort from the fact that God the Father will continue the work begun in them with a view to bringing them to full maturity.

INTERACTION

1. As we conclude our study of the book of Jonah, let us turn again to the familiar story of the prodigal son (Luke 15:11-24). As we consider this well-known narrative, let us focus the spotlight of our attention on the prodigal's father. Think of his heart's response (a) when his son first spoke to him and told him of his desire to leave home, (b) at the time his son left home, (c) during the long months of watching and waiting, and (d) when his son returned.

2. What might have been the father's feelings as his son made his request known and prepared to leave? Are we

as willing when our children grow older to "turn them loose" and give them the opportunity to express their independence and learn from their mistakes? Is there something in the example of this father that will help us trust our sons and daughters to God's loving care when the time comes for them to "leave the nest"? Does God's handling of Jonah offer a source of hope and faith in such a case?

3. What was the father's attitude and pattern of conduct during his son's absence? Is there any evidence of confidence that the training he had given his son and the value system he had imparted to him would bear fruit? On what grounds might we share his confidence?

4. What can we learn about total and unconditional forgiveness from the father's response to his son? What parallels do we see in God's handling of Jonah? What difficulties do we experience when it comes to extending that kind of forgiveness to our children?

5. The son's self-judgment, his "coming to himself" suggests parental training in mature self-evaluation. How can we help our children learn to be appropriately self-appraising so that they need not endure the judgment of others (i.e., God, or society)? What truths are there for us to discover concerning our relationship to God in the son's words: "I am no longer worthy to be called your son" and the father's response? What affirmation of

sonship was offered and what do these (i.e., the robe, ring, shoes) portray of God's acceptance, love and grace? How can we give affirmation to our children concerning their special place in our lives?

NOTES

Chapter 9

WHEN GOD SAYS ENOUGH

As we continue our investigation of what happened to the Assyrians, it is necessary for us to turn the pages of our Bibles from Jonah, past Micah, to Nahum. Here we find that the biographical material of the Book of Jonah gives way to poetry; and the historic narrative is replaced by prophetic imagery. The challenge to us is to master the contents of God's Word concerning Nineveh's downfall and then apply what we learn to our everyday lives. This is not as hard as it may seem. As we do so we will find an abundance of useful information on how *we* may avoid the pitfalls of our willful disobedience while also guiding our sons and daughters toward responsible adulthood.

The book of Nahum was probably written between 668/7 and 654 B.C., about 120 years after Jonah's memoirs.[1] It has two messages: The one conveying comfort to the oppressed (*viz.*, Judah), and the other portraying the consequences of disobedience (addressed to Assyria).

From the practical application of Nahum's "oracle" to our times, we learn that God is personally involved in all that happens to us and uses even the evil about us to work for our good. The value of this information is readily evident: As with those in Judah, we can learn from Nahum how to face the world system and handle the iniquities of life. What he wrote also encourages us to trust in the Lord and do what is right, even when everything seems to be going wrong. And, as we shall see, when these truths are applied to the task of parenthood, we come to understand how Nahum's message can help us direct the progress of our children.

But the vision of Nahum is also one of condemnation. Actions have consequences. No man or nation is an island.

---

1. In determining the date of Nahum's prophecy, two key factors need to be borne in mind. First, Nineveh was still in its heyday when Nahum uttered his warning. From the text, we are given a description of the city bathing in grandeur and might. She is lord of the empires and ready to crush any rebellion beneath her iron heel. This would place the writing of Nahum *before* the reign of Josiah, king of Judah (639-609 B.C.), for by that time the Assyrian empire, with Nineveh as its capital, had begun to lose her grip on the territories to the west. We also know that Nineveh's decline set in after the death of Ashurbanipal (c. 633 B.C.). The book, therefore, must have been penned prior to this date. Second, a further clue to the time of Nahum's "oracle" may be found in his mention of the overthrow and destruction of the Egyptian city of Thebes (3:8-10). From secular history, we know that this took place in 668-67 B.C. In 654 B.C., Thebes began to rise from its ruins. Inasmuch as God saw fit to use the demise of Thebes to illustrate the destruction that would overtake Nineveh–even predicting that the proud city of Nineveh would never be rebuilt–Nahum must have prophesied before 654 B.C., or approximately 120 years after Jonah's ministry (and 40 years before Nineveh was destroyed, 612 B.C.).

What we are individually and nationally affects others. The good or evil that we do has far-reaching effects and, in the final analysis, each one of us is responsible for our own conduct.

These, then, are a few of the practical lessons we will uncover as we probe the message God gave His servant, Nahum. However, one must first inquire into what had happened in Nineveh after Jonah's ministry there.

Advance of the Centuries

Jonah's ministry to Nineveh took place around 785 B.C., soon after Jeroboam II had ascended the throne of Israel and while Adad-nirari III reigned over Assyria. The kings who governed Assyria following Jonah's ministry were greatly feared for their cruelty. They vaunted their savagery in inscriptions carved into rock. Captive monarchs were flayed alive and pillars were clothed with their bleeding flesh. Prisoners of war were walled up, or else impaled on stakes for all to see. The eyes of young men were gouged out; hands, feet, noses and ears were cut off; and huge conflagrations were made where boys and girls were thrown screaming into the flames.[2]

---

2. See F. W. Farrar, *The Minor Prophets* (London: Griffiths, 1907), pp. 144-48.

When, in 722 B.C., the northern tribes of Israel were taken into captivity by the Assyrians, Judah alone was left to feel successively the oppressive hand of Sargon II (722-705 B.C.; cf. Isaiah 20:1), Sennacherib (705-681 B.C.; cf. 2 Kings 18:9--19:37), Esarhaddon (681-669 B.C.; cf. 2 Kings 19:37; Isaiah 37:28) and Ashurbanipal (669-633 B.C.; cf. Ezra 4:10). These years of Assyrian supremacy were ones in which the city of Nineveh was strengthened and embellished more than any other city since the dawn of civilization. Inside the city were parks, botanical gardens and a zoo; and the king boasted of a library of more than 17,000 clay tablets. Palaces were built by the different monarchs; sculptured walls depicted their exploits; conduits brought fresh water from springs thirty miles away, and an aqueduct was constructed to control the flooding of one of the nearby rivers.[3] The wall around Nineveh was enlarged and strengthened. Xenophon, an ancient Greek historian, stated that it was 50 feet thick, 100 feet high, surrounded by moats 150 feet wide and protected by 1200 towers. As a city, therefore, Nineveh was impregnable--or so the Ninevites thought.

In spite of all this grandeur and power, Nineveh was destined to be swept away. The first century (B.C.) historian, Diodorus Siculus, refers to a legend which stated that the city would not be taken until the river became its enemy (cf. Nahum 1:8; 2:6, 3:13,15).

---

3. See Layard, *Nineveh and Babylon* (1853).

Whispers in the Wind

With this brief resume of the facts, we are now ready to take a closer look at the book of Nahum. After long years of oppression there comes to those in Jerusalem a message of comfort. God, speaking through His messenger, tells those in Judah that the time of their testing is over. The Assyrians will oppress them no more.

But politicians, eyeing the tempest of international affairs, pay scant attention to Nahum's prophecy. And those in the imperial city of Nineveh, flushed with their recent victory over Thebes (called No-Amon in 3:8), regard Nahum's message as little more than a whisper in the wind. God, however, in grace, gives the people of Nineveh an entire generation in which to repent.

In announcing God's message, Nahum stresses the eternal realities that all who are self-willed would just as soon forget. God is sovereign. He rules the hearts of all people and exercises Lordship over history. And while He is slow to anger (Jonah 4:2), He will by no means acquit the guilty (Nahum 1:2). All people and nations, therefore, are accountable to Him.

Looking at these divine principles of accountability and judgment (but from a humanistic perspective), Dr. Arnold Toynbee observed that all human cultures grow around a central core of moral ideas and ideals which command obedience, respect and general observance. There is right and there is wrong, both of which are unquestioned. This is what is called the ethos or culture of a people.[4] And these principles of right and wrong have not changed. People and nations are blessed as they live up to the light God has given them and walk in submission to His Word.

Review

But who was Nahum? Where and when did he live? And what did he do?

Nahum's name means "full of comfort," and the vision which he saw of the overthrow of Nineveh was designed to encourage those in Judah to continue to trust in and serve the Lord. From Scripture we glean the fact that Nahum was from Elkosh, a city or village about which nothing definite is known. Some writers favor linking this city or village with Al-Kush, a place twenty-four miles north of Nineveh. Others believe it to be Elcesei, a village in southern Judah. And then there are those who believe Elkosh was an early name for the village which later became Capernaum, *Kaphar-nahum,* "the village of Nahum."

Nahum's style of writing is both poetic and prophetic. He combines lively pictorial imagery with a blunt preview of God's righteous judgment. His writing captivates the

---

4. A. Toynbee, *The Study of History* (New York: McGraw-Hill, 1972).

imagination. Even in his repetition of specific themes there is an unfolding of the grandeur of God's design, a brilliance of description that enriches the text, and an abundance of metaphors that animates his message and adequately communicates God's plan and purpose.

The Answer of History.--Nahum's message is vitally related to the person of God the Father. He is the One in whom Judah is to find consolation when the pressures of circumstances seem overwhelming. He is also the One who will deal with the evil and the good in terms of His righteousness (1:2-6).

In this connection, part of growth toward maturity is realizing that we are responsible to God for what we *do* (John 3:19-21; Romans 2:6) and *say* (Matthew 12:36). There are principles, or absolutes, that govern the attitudes and conduct of individuals and nations, and any deviation from them brings with it its own penalty. Those who learn to obey these principles live in freedom and enjoy the blessing of the Lord upon their lives. Those who do not must bear the consequences of their actions. All of this--the promise of ultimate blessing or the certainty of eventual punishment--is based upon the character of God. And what follows in Nahum's prophecy (1:7-15) shows how the Lord of the universe distinguishes between those who acknowledge His right to direct their lives, and those who say in effect, "We want to run our lives our way" (cf. Luke 19:14, 27; see also Romans 1:18-32; 3:23).

When this truth of cause and effect and actions and consequences is applied to the rearing of children, all of us would have to admit that at one time or another we have encountered the problem God the Father faced with both Judah and Assyria. We naturally want the best for our sons and daughters and sometimes lament that if only they would obey us, things would run smoothly.[5] There seems to be a gap, therefore, between their intention and their performance (cf. Matthew 21:28-29). And it is the same with God the Father. If we, as His children, would only obey Him, we would continue to enjoy His blessing. Because we frequently choose to go our own way and disobey Him, He must chasten us. Only after we have been disciplined by the process He chooses to use does this yield a harvest of righteousness and peace (Hebrews 12:5-11).

Through our study of chapter 1, therefore, we will learn that God the Father is not indifferent to our needs, even as He was not indifferent to Judah's needs. While the process of bringing us to maturity may, at times, be painful, He is not a capricious, unreasonable Parent. He operates on the basis of His love and shows His goodness and compassion to those who come to Him for help (Psalm 46:1).

---

5. See Deuteronomy 4:1-2, 4, 6; 10:12-13; 11:22, 26-28; Joshua 22:5; 23:6; 24:14; 1 Samuel 15:22, 24; 1 Chronicles 28:7, 9; Ezra 7:23; Luke 6:46-48; John 13:17; 14:15, 21, 23; 15:8-10, 14; etc.

Swift Turnabout.--After having considered who God is, we focus our thoughts (in chapter 2) on what Nineveh was like. Nahum pictures God's judgment as if it has already taken place. He describes panic on every hand. The city is surrounded. Flight is useless. There is no escape. God's retributive justice has fallen. The predicted overthrow of Nineveh seemed to be long delayed, but to paraphrase the familiar words of the Greek poet, Euripides, "Though the mills of God['s judgment] grind slowly, yet they grind exceedingly small." He judges righteously and impartially. All attempts to thwart Him or outmaneuver Him are doomed to fail (2:1-13).

All of this brings to mind God's words through Jeremiah, "I will bring upon this people the fruit of their thoughts" (Jeremiah 6:19). Those who have sown to the wind now reap the whirlwind (Hosea 8:7a; cf. 10:12), and those who have lived by the sword will die by the sword (Matthew 26:52).

In this connection, God's awareness of the action He will take is in marked contrast to that of many modern parents. Baffled over how to rear their children, and confused over appropriate methods of discipline, they resort to threats: "You'd better watch out if you know what's good for you," or, "I don't know what I'm going to do, but I'm going to do something if you don't stop doing that right now." In actions such as these they betray their insecurity and unconsciously show their sons and daughters that they are uncomfortable in their role as parents.

In forewarning Nineveh, God announced His intention to punish the nation. There was no indecision on His part. During the interval between the proclamation of His intent through Nahum and the overthrow of the capital, individuals were given approximately one generation in which to repent and leave the city.[6] All of this highlights God's love and grace on the one hand and illustrates the difference between corporate and individual punishment on the other. The nation was under judgment, but those within it still had time to turn from their evil ways and seek the Lord. This principle is borne out in history. When the cities of Sodom and Gomorrah were overthrown, God plainly promised Abraham that if there were ten righteous people in the city, He would spare the many for the sake of the few (Genesis 18:20-33). Only Lot and his family (as individuals) were found righteous, and they were taken from the city (the corporate entity) before it was destroyed (Genesis 19: 23-26).

According to Eusebius (A.D. 260-340), one of the earliest Christian historians, when Jerusalem was attacked in A.D. 70 by the Roman general, Titus, the Christians were warned of the destruction of the city through reading Matthew 24:15-16. They fled to Pella, a city in Perea (Trans Jor-

---

6. Shortly before the predicted events were scheduled to take place, another warning was given, this time through Zephaniah (Zephaniah 2:13-15). His message was designed to rekindle hope in Judah and also reawaken the consciences of those in Assyria who either had not heard or had forgotten the message of Nahum.

dan), and were spared the destruction which overtook those who remained within Jerusalem.[7] Here, in the wisdom and grace of God, Nahum serves as His messenger to warn the people of Nineveh of the consequences of their deeds and the reality of their judgment. Those who might heed his warning have time to repent.

Day of the Coup.--Finally, in chapter 3, we read about Nineveh's demise. God shows us that His moral law will be upheld. Retribution will be in kind. Those who murdered the innocent and the helpless are to be made desolate without mercy (3:1-3). Those who gloried in their immoral practices are to be treated in like manner (3:4-7). As they had treated Thebes, so they will be treated (3:8-10). Resistance will be useless. Their carefully laid plans for defense will fail. Their armies will desert the city and the inhabitants will be scattered, never to be regathered (3:11-18). And those who have been oppressed will rejoice at Nineveh's fall (3:19).

Even in this section there are important principles of parenthood. A solemn responsibility is placed on us as parents to help our sons and daughters review the direction of their lives. Teenagers are particularly susceptible to peer pressure. Their friends exert tremendous influence upon

---

7. See *The Ecclesiastical History of Eusebius Pamphilus* (Grand Rapids: Baker, 1962), pp. 93-94.

them and can easily govern their dress, speech, moral standards and social attitudes.

In the adolescent years less control is preferable to tight control. Discipline, however, is more effective when it includes a rationale. In the case of Nineveh, God says in effect, "You see yourselves as grown up and able to make your own decisions. Let me give you a rationale for My behavior. You have willingly and deliberately broken My moral law. Now this is what I am going to do." He does not stand by silently watching and then suddenly pounce on them. He warns them in advance, giving them a reason for His actions and allowing them to make their own decisions.

Parents sometimes find that their sons and daughters go through a stage in which they discard the values in which they have been reared and embrace other standards. Their response to any remonstrance may be, "That's fine for you, Mom and Dad. What you want me to do used to be the accepted thing when you were young, but the world is changing. We have to keep up with the times or be left behind. I'd rather live my life by different standards. For you to insist that I hold to your system of values is presumptuous. How do you know that yours is right?"

From a careful consideration of chapter 3, we find God saying in effect, "Cultural values may change, but principles of right and wrong do not. My system of values is based on timeless absolutes. These apply to all segments of society regardless of current mores. Appropriate conduct is in keeping with these absolutes. Those who obey Me enjoy My blessing. Those who disobey Me must be prepared to face the consequences of breaking My law."

How much better, therefore, as our sons and daughters approach adulthood, for us to encourage them to take direction from their divine Parent, and, by following His standards, continue to grow towards full maturity. By doing so, they will enjoy His blessing all their lives.

INTERACTION

1. Throughout Scripture we observe patterns of God's conduct; namely, that God's promises tend to be made well in advance of their fulfillment. Knowing the human tendency to desire immediate fulfillment of our needs and wants, is it possible that through delay God gives us opportunity to learn patience and postpone gratification (a critical dimension of adult maturity)? How can we, as parents, help our children learn that all their needs and desires will not be granted immediately, and that if they were, this would only tend to perpetuate their infantile expectations?

2. Little Michael, having been told by his mother that he cannot have a cookie until after dinner, can't bear to wait. He slips into the kitchen while her back is turned and reaches up for the cookie jar. Unfortunately for

him, he only succeeds in pulling the jar off the sideboard onto the floor where it breaks. Obviously, his mother cannot ignore the clatter and administers some appropriate discipline which includes picking up the pieces of the broken jar, and a "swat" on his bottom. Meanwhile, Michael's fourteen-year-old sister, Judy, has been admonished by her parents at breakfast to see to a tidier room. We find her parents delaying their discipline to give Judy an opportunity to consider their request and assume responsibility for her room through her own planning rather than totally directing her as they would little Michael. Discuss examples from the Bible where God delayed His discipline to give those concerned the opportunity to be responsible. How might we apply this concept (a) to ourselves and (b) to our children of different ages?

3. In God's dealings with both Judah and Nineveh, we are reminded again of the consistency of His love and righteousness, His patience and discretion, His understanding and expectations. We observe that, as they obeyed God, they enjoyed the blessings of His love, and as they did not, they experienced His discipline or punishment. How might we, as parents, emulate God's divine model as we relate to our children in a balanced and considerate fashion? What are the specific attributes we would wish to apply? Think of examples of both success and failure in following God's pattern that you might share with one another.

4. In 2 Timothy 3:16 we are informed of the great value of God's Word in our lives. Nineveh had the opportunity to experience this value both through the preaching of Jonah and through the prophecy of Nahum. We are aware, however, of her failure to ultimately profit from God's forbearance (Romans 2:4). Following Jonah's ministry we do not read of any heart-hunger for the Word (1 Peter 2:2). Hebrews 5:13-14 points out clearly the place of the Word of God in growth towards maturity. How may we instill in our children (a) a desire for God's Word and (b) a willingness to obey its teaching?

5. In what ways may we distinguish between God's eternal absolutes expressed in His Word and our own cultural mores? What should be our response to the conduct of our sons and daughters as it relates to each of these sets of standards? Discuss this issue in light of the authoritarian, authoritative and permissive models of parenting.

NOTES

Chapter 10

NO LAUGHING MATTER

Several years ago the renowned child psychologist Erik Erikson stated that "there is in every child at every stage [in his or her development] a new miracle of vigorous unfolding, which constitutes new hope and a new responsibility." During adolescence and young adulthood, this growth involves the establishment of a sense of identity separate from one's parents so that the emerging young man or woman can create and maintain intimate relationships of their own. It is at this time that the kind of parenting they have received--whether authoritarian, authoritative, or permissive--becomes apparent in their behavior.

Different Families, Different Worries

Let us listen in on a conversation over coffee at a neighbor's house one morning. A mother is telling the others about her teenage son. She describes his latest rebellion and laments that "all he wants to do is take the family car and go off with his friends. Only last week he was involved in an accident--a minor one--and now his father has forbidden him the use of the car." She continues by describing her son's sullen defiance and fears that he and his father will again become involved in a heated argument.

And the reason? This young man's home environment has been harsh and demanding. In a word, authoritarian. His social development has been stifled. He feels unaccepted and controlled by his parents, and is now reacting against all forms of authority. His outward conduct appears irresponsible. He equates "happiness" with being away from home with those who feel the way he does. He and his friends believe that they are misunderstood. They are confused and tend to isolate themselves more and more from those whom they feel have rejected them.

Or, consider the case of a man in his mid-forties. He has a teenage daughter who is the idol of his life. He and his wife have always given her everything she ever wanted. She is now in her senior year at high school. As with other teenagers her age, she has felt the pressure of her peers and has recently begun keeping company with some of those who were formerly her upper classmates and are now college freshmen. She is flattered by their attention and very impressed with their (supposed) sophistication. When her parents try to warn her of certain social dangers, she turns on them in anger. Her father is crushed by this display of "disrespect" and pleads weakly with her to give them a hearing.

But why has there come about a change in this young girl's attitude? Her parents have always behaved in a non-punitive and accepting way. They have tolerated her actions and desires. Few demands have been made upon her. Controls have been minimal. She has been allowed to regulate her own life and activities. With such permissive training, their daughter has developed a poor attitude toward authority. Outwardly she appears self--indulgent and irresponsible. Inwardly she has become hostile for not having proper restraints placed upon her; and now, when her will has clashed with the desires of her parents, she is in open rebellion.

An individual's personality develops positively or negatively in relation to his or her consistent exposure to good or bad relations with other significant people (and in particular, one's parents). This is especially true when a child perceives the parent(s) as being emotionally detached, aloof and unresponsive (i.e., permissive), or unloving and persecuting (i.e., authoritarian). The result is insecurity, a high degree of dependence upon others, absence of principles, and little sense of inner direction.

Forever Tainted

As we probe Nahum's indictment of Nineveh, we discover that the polarities of authoritarianism and permissiveness find their place in Assyrian life and culture. Discipline was very strict. The training of the youth, whether in the army, the schools (called "tablet houses"), the trades or the professions, was very rigorous. Punishment, even for minor offenses, was severe. Such rigidity fostered its own forms of hostility.

The religious beliefs of the Assyrians furthered their aggression. The principal deity, Ashur, was the god of war. He was very distant from the people, but very powerful. And then there was Inanna, goddess of sex and defender of warriors. Her worship was very permissive and, of course, she was very popular.[1] Religious prostitution was practiced in her name.

These elements of authoritarianism and permissiveness were joined together in their culture in much the same way that in many homes one parent is harsh and demanding while the other allows the children to virtually rear themselves. But the hostility which these models generate is invariably acted out in a self-indulgent way. Resentment against all forms of authority, oppression of others, and immoral behavior are the natural result.

---

1. Ashur, god of war, was the principal deity of the Assyrians. The campaigns of the Assyrians were believed to be "holy wars" against those who failed to submit to Ashur's sovereignty. His primary temple was at Assur. The reigning monarchs made much of him (in order to further their own plans for war), but the common people preferred the more sensual worship of Inanna. Inanna (or Ishtar), goddess of war and fertility, was the devoted deity of Nineveh. Her worship was very permissive. Nabu (or Nebo), god of wisdom and patron of the sciences, had temples at both Nineveh and Calah. For further information, see A. T. Olmstead, *History of Assyria* (Chicago: University of Chicago Press, 1964), and G. van Driel, *The Cult of Assur* (Assen, The Netherlands: Van Gorcum, 1969).

With the realization that certain trends in Assyrian culture parallel our own, we may look more closely at Nahum's message to glean from it principles for our own life and conduct. Consider, for example, how we, as a nation, have lost sight of the principles of morality and human dignity that God planted in the heart of every man. Our decline in standards of right conduct has touched every aspect of our lives and has led to widespread dishonesty, violence, deceit, and the belief that "the end justifies the means." Coupled with this decline in morals is an increase in technology that has served to further decrease one's personal worth, causing the rank and file of humanity to feel that they are exploited.[2] They then feel that they must seek safety and fulfillment in schemes or plans of their own. This has intensified the "cult" of individualism that demands that each person create his or her own world by self-direction, self-realization and self-fulfillment.

With these forces operating in our society, it is difficult to find an effective approach to counteract the problems generated by these changes. We have become insensitive to the subtleties of moral discrimination and now place a high premium on personal experience. We have given ourselves over to pleasure and put God's principles behind our backs.

---

2. We are prone to define "*immorality*" in sexual terms. In reality, *immorality* occurs whenever people are treated as things, and things are invested with the worth that rightly belongs to people.

And when these false approaches to life are reproduced in our children, the result is tragic indeed!

It is therefore most important for us to learn from Assyria's experience. God does not change from age to age, and the principles that He has chosen to reveal to us should be heeded if we are to avoid Assyria's fate.

Undeniable Reality

In penning the weighty[3] matters that make up his vision, Nahum speaks as if the calamities he predicts have taken place already. His opening words are startling: "A jealous and an avenging *'El* (God, the all-powerful) is the *Yahweh* (the LORD); *Yahweh* (the LORD) is avenging and wrathful [lit., full of heat]. *Yahweh* (the LORD) takes vengeance against His adversaries, and He keeps His [wrath] for His enemies. *Yahweh* (the LORD) is slow to anger and great in power, and *Yahweh* (the LORD) will by no means leave the guilty unpunished."

The strong emphasis on *Yahweh*, "LORD," in these opening verses cannot be overlooked. Whether the Assyrians wish to believe it or not, they are accountable to Him.

---

3. The term used in the biblical text is "burden" (sometimes translated "oracle" as in 1:1). It is frequently found in prophetic inscriptions (cf. Isaiah 13:1; Zechariah 12:1; Habakkuk 1:1; Malachi 1:1), and implies "to lift" a heavy object. When applied to prophecy, it denotes a solemn, weighty or burdensome theme.

He is Sovereign. He is the One before whom all their deeds have been performed. Now, according to Nahum's prediction, they are to give an account of their actions to Him.

The opening description of God is as instructive as it is awe-inspiring. Nahum describes Him as "jealous and avenging." To us, jealousy conjures up thoughts of suspicion, distrust and fear of rivalry. When applied to God, however, jealousy embodies the idea of His unreserved claim to the love and devotion of all members of His creation. He will tolerate no rival. He requires the perfect love, reverence and trust of His creatures. He is anxious for their good, angered by their sinfulness and intolerant of all substitute deities. This emotion (i.e., His jealousy) is closely allied with His will. He also is avenging--executing judgment on His enemies, vindicating His honor, and justifying those who trust in Him.

As a "Parent," God is *authoritative*. He does not suppress His anger. When a parent suppresses anger, a child thinks that he or she has been able to get away with his or her misbehavior. Unfortunately, suppressed anger has a habit of erupting. Sooner or later we lose control. We then feel guilty for our loss of temper and try to make amends. This confuses our child. Just when he or she is beginning to learn from the experience, there is a change in the parental attitude that appears to call everything back.

Anger is legitimate when expressed in a controlled way and when directed against something that is wrong. Paul instructed the believers in his day to "be angry and not sin" (Ephesians 4:26; see also Proverbs 15:1; 16:32; 19:11,19; 25:28; 29:8-9, 22). There is no excuse, however, for one's anger to spill over in all directions. Balance is required. As we consider the example of the Lord Jesus Christ, we find that there were occasions in His earthly life when He was angry (Mark 3:5; cf. John 3: 13-17). His anger was always focused on the object rather than on the subject. Vengeance, however, is the prerogative of almighty God (Deuteronomy 32:35, 41, 43; Psalm 94:1; Romans 12:19).

Nahum's description of God the Father as "slow to anger and great in power," and One who will "by no means leave the guilty unpunished," is likewise full of instruction. His mercy and His power meet together. He is aware of our frailty. And, while He is the only One who is really all-powerful (i.e., omnipotent), we should recognize something of our "omnipotence" where our children are concerned. We appear to be of great power to them. In dealing with them we should follow the example of our heavenly Father and be slow to anger, authoritative in dealing with them, kind--yet uncompromising--balanced in our judgment, and ever mindful of the fact that our actions will have far-reaching effects on their lives.

Doomsday Scenario

But those in Nineveh who pay attention to Nahum's words might ask, "Does this God have the power to carry out what He has promised? It's one thing to claim to have power, but what demonstration of His might can He point to? We have overrun every nation from the Persian Gulf in the east to the Great Sea (the Mediterranean) in the west. Have the gods of these nations been able to help them against us? Who, then, is Yahweh that we should listen to Him?"

In verses 3*b*-7 Nahum describes the power and the authority of the Lord. Man at best can predict the weather, but He has His way in the whirlwind and the storm. The clouds are as dust beneath His feet. He is able to rebuke the sea and make it dry (cf. Exodus 14:21-31: Joshua 3:7-17); and He can make the most fertile places a barren waste. Mountains are moved and the earth is in upheaval at His presence. "Who can stand before His indignation?" Nahum asks, "Who can endure the burning of His anger?" The answer to these rhetorical questions is obvious: "No one." And yet, God delays executing His wrath against sin because of His mercy. He grants people the opportunity to repent. As the apostle Peter pointed out, "The Lord is not slow in keeping His promises as some believe. He is patient and longsuffering . . . not purposing that any should perish but that all men should come to repentance" (2 Peter 3:9).

In Nahum's panoramic portrayal of God's power, there is also an element of comfort. He points out that "the LORD is good, a stronghold in the day of trouble, and He knows those who take refuge in Him." Here is God's offer of mercy. Here is His "evangelistic" appeal. This truth gives all who trust in Him--whether Assyria, Judah, or us--a real sense of security. It also adds a balanced perspective to life. As with Assyrians, we are in danger of adopting the false view that the here and now is all that really matters. We tend to subscribe to the theory that "we only go around once in life," and that we must "reach for all the gusto we can get." Such a pleasure-seeking outlook breeds insecurity, for when deprived of that which satisfies the desires of our senses, when faced with sudden adversity or confronted with the inequities of life, we lose confidence in the present and have no hope for the future.

By way of contrast, Nahum emphasizes a fact later developed in the book of Hebrews (11:13-16), that this life is merely a preparation for eternity. Whatever comes our way of good or evil is designed to help us become what God intends. Such a belief opens us to growth and development towards true maturity. In the New Testament, this teaching is expanded to include conformity to the image of Christ (e.g., Ephesians 4:15; Colossians 2:7; 1 Peter 2:2, 5; 2 Peter 3:18).

This is illustrated for us in a most interesting way. A young man, whose girl friend lived in a distant city, wanted to have an engagement ring on hand when he proposed to her. He sought the help of a friend who was a jeweler. In due course, after designing the ring, he was shown the materials. The diamond looked like any other stone he might have seen in a garden or along a sidewalk. And the gold was a bright garish color, not at all like the gold he had seen used in other jewelry. On questioning the jeweler about the gold, he was told that it had not yet been purified or refined. Still in doubt about the eventual beauty of the engagement ring, he asked: "And how do you know when it is pure enough?" To which the jeweler replied as he peered over the crucible, "When I can see my face in it."

This is God's intent for us. He allows the purifying fires of adversity to purge out the dross so that we may reflect the moral glory of Christ.

The Way It Will Be

From this general statement of God's plan--a statement that has alternated between His attitude toward the Ninevites and His compassion for those in Judah--Nahum moves to the specifics.[4] He has described who God is. Now he portrays what he will do. Apparently Nahum saw those in Nineveh taking counsel on how to thwart God's plan. From

---

4. A theory propounded by the late Robert Pfeiffer of Harvard University sought to find an alphabetic (or acrostic) psalm in 1:2-10. Because the text did not follow the order of the letters of the Hebrew alphabet, and also was incomplete, Pfeiffer first rearranged the verses (placing them in order as follows: 1, 10, 3, 5, 12, 9, 6, 13 and 11). And where there were no verses beginning with a letter of the Hebrew alphabet, he assumed that they had been lost in emendation or through textual corruption. Such a view totally distorts the sequence of thought in these verses. As it stands, Nahum's prediction makes perfect sense.

an earthly perspective, they were developing a strategy to combat the Medes and Babylonians, but in reality they are viewed as resisting the Lord. Nahum promises them that God's judgment will be so thorough that it will not have to be repeated (Nahum 1:12). Those who trust in the strength of Nineveh's walls and imagine themselves safe behind her seemingly impregnable ramparts or in her towers will find that their confidence has been misplaced. Such is always the lot of those who trust in earthly things.

In this respect, the Assyrians were little different from people today. We strive from birth to become independent and self-sufficient. In the words of William Henley's *Invictus*, we want to be able to say,

> I am the master of my fate;
> I am the captain of my soul.

Eve cradled this desire in her heart at the time of the Fall. She wanted to be "like God" (Genesis 3:5) --knowing good and evil, and answerable to no one. This was the sin the devil himself had committed (Isaiah 14:13-14). He wanted equal status with God so that he could be independent of Him. We call this desire "pride." It is, in reality, a striving for omnipotence and sovereignty. We want to control our own world.

But pride breeds arrogance, and these twin evils were prominent in the character of the Assyrian kings. As proof of this, Nahum points to the fact that "from [Nineveh] has gone forth one who plotted evil against *Yahweh* (the LORD) ...." His statement is generally believed to refer to Sennacherib, who warred against Judah in the days of Hezekiah (2 Kings 18:13-19:37). But Sennacherib's vast army had met with defeat at the hands of the "angel of the LORD" in 701 B.C. (2 Kings 19:35). It seems preferable to conclude that Nahum is using a figure of speech that personifies either the nation or their principal god, Ashur, on whose behalf all their wars were fought. Such an explanation takes into consideration the fact that Assyria's aggression is spoken of as being directed "against the LORD" (1:9).

This desire for power and autonomy manifests itself in our children at an early age. They try to manipulate people and circumstances in order to get their own way. The challenge to us as parents is to recognize their basic need for confidence and provide for success experiences. Such provision will tend to minimize the power-struggles that develop when a child lacks confidence and a feeling of accomplishment. It will also provide a climate conducive to the growth of their individual capacities. Such an environment should also demonstrate the practicality of submission to the will of God and be vitally linked with a desire to learn more of His ways as we recognize that our ultimate security lies in His sufficiency rather than our own. True maturity begins when we cease from our own striving for power and control, and surrender ourselves to His authority. Then, instead of becoming passive response systems, we actively engage in serving Him in all we do.

Comfort and Hope

But there is more. Nahum's message also clarifies the issues for those living in Judah who, on account of the prevailing spiritual laxity, may not have been aware of the reason for their subjection. Throughout their history, God had appointed messengers to reprove His people for their sins and call them back to Himself. Over the years the people had grown dull of hearing. Now He speaks to them again, this time through Nahum. He says in effect, "I did it. I allowed you to be afflicted. I did it for your good--to wean you away from the error of your ways. Now the time of chastening is over" (Nahum 1:12*b*-13). In other words, when God disciplines His own, there is a clear application accompanied by an appropriate termination. His message is one of comfort. The false gods of Assyria are to be destroyed. So complete will be Nineveh's destruction that it will never again rise from its ruins (Nahum1:14). Those within the city will suffer the same fate. There will be no posterity. What they have sown they are now about to reap.

It is significant that, not long after Nahum's words, Assyrian power began to crumble. Rebellion within the empire reduced its strength. Subject nations refused to pay tribute. In 614 B.C. Cyaxares, king of the Medes, invaded Assyria. He was repulsed, but two years later, with his army augmented by forces from Babylon, he renewed the attack. Finally, the proud, impregnable city fell. Nahum's prophecy was so completely fulfilled that years later, when Alexander the Great marched his armies over the site, he was unaware that beneath their feet lay the once mighty "mistress" of the ancient Near East.

So sure is God's word of fulfillment that Nahum sees, as it were, a runner (or messenger) bringing news of the overthrow of Assyria to those in Jerusalem. "Look!" he exclaims. "There on the mountains is the one who, fleet of foot, is bringing good news--a message of peace! Celebrate your feasts, O Judah; pay your vows, for never again will the worthless one pass through you; he is cut off completely." The days of tyranny are ended; deliverance has come. The people are to rejoice in faith believing that what God has promised will come to pass. And they are encouraged to fulfill their promises made to the Lord during their time of oppression.

In this closing scene, God the Father shows Himself to be a loving, authoritative Parent. He directs His "children's" (i.e., Judah's) activities in a rational, issue-oriented way. He encourages their self--expression ("rejoicing"), and His reason behind the "celebration" is willingly shared. He shows that He values their autonomous self-will and their self-discipline (the "paying of their vows"). In the past He has exercised firm control at points of "Parent-child" divergence, but at no time have those in Judah been hemmed in with restrictions. Both His rights and their interests have been recognized. Even when they transgressed His covenant, He demonstrated time and again His affection for and free acceptance of them. And now, as they face the future unclouded by Assyrian domination, He encourages them to live up to His standards without loss of individual autonomy.

Such parenting demonstrates a warm, rational, receptive approach; communicates positive, loving safeguards; and also encourages independent striving. It cultivates self-reliance and self-control, and produces personally content, happy young men and women who are able to progress toward maturity.

INTERACTION

In considering the authoritarian, permissive and authoritative models of parenting, analyze the characteristics, values and consequences of each. The following charts and descriptions may prove helpful.

1. *The authoritarian parent* is characterized as attempting to shape, control and evaluate the child's behavior and attitudes according to a set standard of conduct (usually an absolute standard). Obedience is considered a primary virtue while punitive, forceful means are used to curb the child's expression of self-will in areas where his behavior or beliefs conflict with what is considered proper conduct. Verbal give and take is not encouraged. Rather, the child is expected to accept without question the parent's word as right. This parent can be viewed as

being typically very high on the matter of control, but low in acceptance of the child as a person.

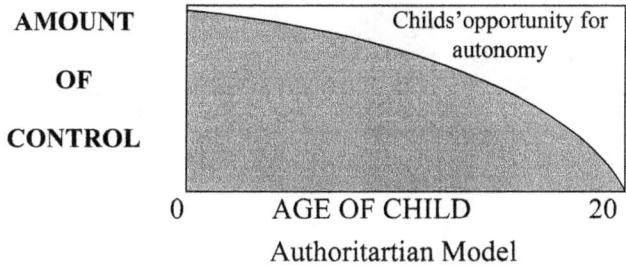
Authoritartian Model

2. *The permissive parent* is viewed as attempting to behave in a nonpunitive, accepting, and affirmative manner toward the child's actions and desires. Few demands are made regarding household behavior or orderly conduct. The permissive parent allows the child to regulate his own activities to as great an extent as possible, avoids exercising control and attempts to employ reason (but not overt power) in accomplishing parental goals. The permissive parent can thus be considered high in acceptance of the child as a person, and low in control.

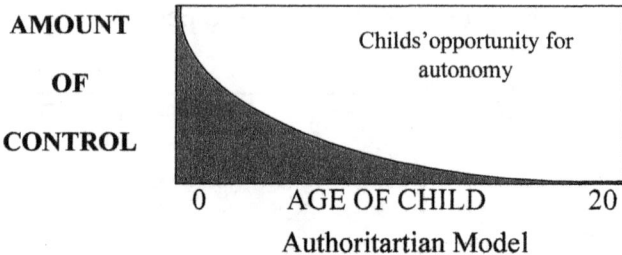

Authoritartian Model

3. *The authoritative parent* is viewed as attempting to actively direct the child's activities but in a manner that is rational and issue-oriented. Verbal give and take is encouraged, and the reasoning behind parental policies is willingly shared with the child. Both autonomous self-will and disciplined conformity are valued. Firm control is exerted at points of parent-child divergence, but the child is not hemmed in with restrictions. Both the parents' special rights as an adult and the child's individual interests and unique characteristics are recognized. The authoritative parent supports the child's present qualities. Acceptance and affection, both physical and verbal, are given freely and are not conditioned on performance. At the same time the parents set standards and have expectations for future conduct. Reason, as well as discipline, is used to achieve parental objectives. Authoritative control can achieve responsible conformity with family and group standards without loss of individual autonomy or self-assertiveness. Typi-

cally, the authoritative parent is high in both acceptance and control.

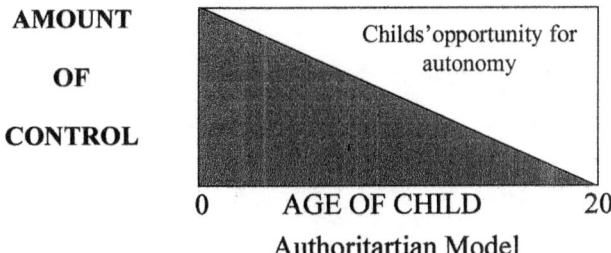

Authoritartian Model

In the light of the above-mentioned models of parenting, (1) What effect will each have on the child's sense of belonging, feeling of worth, and inner confidence? (2) If a child tends to see in his/her parents a reflection of God the Father, what will his/her perception of God be like? (3) And what kinds of behavior will these styles of parenting elicit from the child?

NOTES

Chapter 11

PUTTING PEACE IN PERSPECTIVE

Our previous chapter concluded with glad news being brought to Jerusalem. Victory was at hand. The threat of violence was past. A new day was dawning for those in Judah.

Now, the scene changes. The new vision repeats the first and adds details not found in an earlier chapter. From the description given of the awful arsenal of the Almighty, the focus shifts to the historical consummation of His vengeance. With the vividness of an eyewitness (who saw in a prophetic vision the destruction of Nineveh before it took place), Nahum describes the action. The use of the (prophetic) perfect tense looks at the action as if the events are already a part of history. Nahum depicts in rapid succession the approach of the assailant, the preparations for the attack, the charging of the chariots, the opening of the gates, the flight of the population, the treasures plundered by the captors, and the city which had hitherto been the home of fearless (and ferocious) warriors (described as a "den of lions," see Nahum 2:11ff.), is now deserted and silent.[1]

---

1. Chapter 1:15 in our Bibles is 2:1 in the Hebrew Bible. In this instance the division in our Bibles is preferable. See S. R. Driver, *The Minor Prophets*, The Century Bible (New York: Oxford University Press, 1906), p. 12.

Bitter Fruit

The opening verse recalls to mind the fact that Assyria was the first nation to deport to other lands the people of subject kingdoms (2 Kings 17:23). Now they are to reap what they have sown. "The One who scatters [or dispossesses] has come up against you [lit., before your face]." The prophet affirms that while the Ninevites will see only the armies of the Medes and Chaldeans, the real "Dispossessor" is the Lord. He is working behind the scenes to accomplish His purpose.

Knowing that those in Nineveh will do all they can to protect themselves, Nahum adds a touch of irony to his prediction. "Man the fortress," he says, "watch the road, make strong your loins, strengthen yourselves as much as you can." It is a graphic scene. The enemy is on the way. They will soon appear. The Ninevites, to a man, are to keep a sharp lookout. They are to summon all their strength, and make every preparation for the defense of the city. And when the attack is launched, they are to present as strong and as solid a front as possible.

In reality, their preparations will be in vain, for the Lord is about to restore the splendor of the true sons of Jacob like the splendor of Israel during the Solomonic age.[2] Even though His people, as a vine, have been devastated and their branches destroyed, He is going to renew their greatness. The tables are going to be turned. He will break the yoke of oppression. His people will be freed from those who have devastated them. The "vine" will then grow new branches and bear a "harvest" that will indeed honor the "Vinedresser."[3]

It is easy for us, as we study the biblical text, to become so preoccupied with the vivid imagery of Nahum's prophecy that we overlook the truth that is being presented. God is the One who possesses power and might. He is the One who plants and plucks up. We, as His children, derive our security from Him. It is our responsibility to make the truths of His Word a part of our lives. And when it comes to our children, we take on many of these same attributes. While our children are very young, they think that their mothers are everywhere present and that their fathers are all powerful. To them, the fact that "Mommy is here" means that everything is all right. And when something breaks, their father is the one who can always "fix it."

---

2. The overthrow of Nineveh was partially fulfilled when Assyria, as a nation, could no longer oppress those in Judah. Unfortunately God's people failed to walk in His ways and did not enter into the full measure of the blessings He had in store for them. The ultimate fulfillment of this promise is, therefore, still future.
3. The ultimate fulfillment of this prediction will be in the Millennium. The symbolism of a "vine" representing God's people is found in many passages of the Bible (cf. Psalm 80:13; Isaiah 5:1-7; Jeremiah 2:21; Matthew 21:33-41; John 15:1-6, 16).

In adolescence, however, there comes about a change with the proverbial "cutting of the apron strings" and the breaking of paternal ties. Parents are still around if they are needed, but now a son or daughter is on his or her own. They must now bear the responsibility for their actions. Some, as with Assyria, regrettably will become wayward. They will be intent on serving their own ends. Others, as with those in Judah, will find themselves easily oppressed or exploited. They may rely on their own strength or resourcefulness, only to find that they never seem to be able to rise above their circumstances.

To all of us there comes the assurance that if we examine ourselves in the light of the Scriptures, accept God's offer of pardon and walk in His ways (cf. 1 John 1:5-2:2), we can avoid the judgment of God (1 Corinthians 11:31). This the Assyrians failed to do.

Nahum's words also contain a message of comfort. Those in Judah feel that they have been so long oppressed that life holds nothing better for them than more oppression. The harder they try, the less progress they seem to make. At a time like this, the words of God through His prophet are most consoling. There is no need to despair. If they will only turn to Him, the "branches" can grow again and they can become fruitful in every good work (Colossians 1:10).

This is a truth that also needs to be imparted to our sons and daughters. They, too, need to learn that the path to maturity involves a choice. Those who choose to follow the path of self-will (which Assyria trod--a path which will be elaborated on in our next chapter) must be prepared to face the consequences of their decision. But those who place their confidence in the Lord, "pay their vows" and serve Him, will enjoy His blessing. His word is sure: those who honor Him, will be honored by Him; and those who despise Him will be lightly esteemed (I Samuel 2:3; cf. Matthew 6:33).

When, Not If

With verse 3 the scene changes once more. Whereas the chapter opened with a challenge to Assyria to prepare for invasion and a message of hope to Judah, our attention is now focused on the invaders. They are drawn up in battle array out of sight of the city. The commander-in-chief reviews his troops. The shields of the warriors are stained red, to give the impression that they are covered with blood. The soldiers are attired in scarlet military cloaks, so that they are easily identifiable. Their chariots are made of wood and overlaid with iron or steel. They reflect the rays of the morning sun, giving the onlooker the impression of a blazing fire. To these assembled men, Cyaxares, king of the Medes, accompanied by Nebopolassar, king of the Chaldeans, gives his final challenge. He spurs them on to victory. They respond by brandishing their spears in the air. They are ready for battle.

Once again, the scene shifts. The picture brought before the mind of the reader in verse 4 is now of the battle. The armies of the Medes and Chaldeans (Babylonians) have breached the outer circumference of greater Nineveh's defenses.[4] There is fighting in the plaza areas. The chariots, armed with deadly scythes on their axles, race through the streets cutting down those who are unable to move out of their path. As the charioteers dash from place to place, the brilliance of the sun is reflected from the polished metal. An onlooker might easily liken them to torches igniting fires throughout the city.

When the outer districts of Greater Nineveh have fallen, the attention of the invaders is directed to the walls of the citadel itself. The leader of the main force calls up his nobles and, with them, the best military units. They represent his elite corp. Such is their eagerness that "they stumble in their march." Either they jostle one another in their haste to reach the wall, or, in their eagerness, stumble over their own feet. In any event, on reaching the wall, a "mantled" (cover or shield) is set up so that the soldiers can prepare the scaffold to mount the wall. This mantled is designed to protect them from archers on the wall, boiling oil poured down on them from above or stones thrown from the battlements.[5]

---

4. For a description of Greater Nineveh, see *The Biblical World*, pp. 415-21; and Andre Perrot's *Nineveh and the Old Testament* (London: SCM, 1955), pp. 76-87.

The Irresistible Force

The attackers, however, have been reserving their most powerful weapon for last. Nineveh has experienced flooding in the past. Three rivers, the Tigris, the Khoser and the Tebiltu, either converge near Nineveh, flow parallel to one another or traverse the city. They are part of the network of canals and moats that both irrigate the land and protect the capitol. Dams and sluice gates have been constructed to control flooding. Now the attackers strategically opened these gates and a rushing wall of water causes a section of the rampart to collapse.

The foundations of the walls were of stone, but the walls themselves were of baked brick. It is probable that, following Sennacherib's refortification of the city half a century earlier, the foundations had been settling into the mud. The sudden flood caused a large portion of the wall to collapse. The water then reduced the king's palace to a mass of muddy debris. It time all the buildings were similarly affected. It is no wonder that grass grew quickly over the city, completely hiding it from view.

---

5. See 2 Chronicles 26:11-15. See also H. E. Freeman, *Nahum, Zephaniah, Habakkuk* (Chicago: Moody, 1973), pp. 27-28; Y. Yadin, *The Art of Warfare in Bible Lands*, and the article on "War" in *Zondervan's Pictorial Encyclopedia of the Bible*, V:894-900.

Tale of Horror

A slight interpretive problem arises in verse 7. It concerns the word "she." The key to its solution lies in the usage of the word *huzzah*. The text reads, "And it is *huzzah*: She is stripped, she is carried away, and her handmaids [in mourning] are moaning like the sound of doves, beating on their breasts [i.e., over their hearts]."

Many writers take *huzzah* to be a noun for mistress, or the proper name of the queen of Nineveh. In defense of this view, there was the common practice of kings in ancient times to take captive the women of a city. Those of the royal family would then be stripped naked and paraded before the leaders of the victorious army (cf. Isaiah 47:2-3). To see those who had shared his bed with him degraded and humiliated before his eyes was regarded as the greatest indignity to which a conquered king could be subjected.

If this is the correct view, then we have here an illustration of poetic justice. The manner in which Assyria had dealt with other royal captives is now to be the experience of their queen and her court. And her maids, aware of the fate awaiting them at the hands of ruthless soldiers, give way to expressions of grief and dejection.

The word, *huzzah*, however, can also mean "to make a stand" or "to decree." The former meaning (i.e., of "mistress") does not fit the context, for from verse 8 we know that the inhabitants of the city flee before the invaders. Since in Nahum 1:8 the city is personified as a woman (the translation "its site" is literally "her place"), and in 2:10 the city is again spoken of as "she," we should, to be consistent, interpret 2:7 as a figure of speech used to describe the city. Her downfall is part of God's "decree." This latter interpretation is preferable, for we know that king Sinsharishkun sent his sons and daughters to Paphlagonia for safety before Nineveh was attacked. It seems likely that the queen and certain of the other mothers of the king's children accompanied them, and that only the king's concubines and the palace servants remained with the king in Nineveh (cf. 2 Samuel 15:16).

Ghosts Out of the Past

The collapse of the wall of Nineveh only serves to heighten the panic inside the capital. Water is everywhere. Throughout Nineveh's long history, there has been little to disturb her peace. She has resembled a tranquil pool. The wars fought had invariably been far-removed from the city limits. Now, even the soldiers desert the city. "Stop, stop," shouts an officer; but none obey his command. All are intent on their own safety. No one turns back. Little resistance is offered and the city falls. She is now at the mercy of her captors. And with the fighting over, a commander gives instructions to loot the city. "Plunder the silver! Plunder the gold! For there is no limit to the treasure--wealth of every kind, of every desirable object." Nineveh's great treasures, the result of her many conquests, now become the spoils of war for the conquerors. Palaces, temples, dwellings are all stripped of their wealth. Tacit confirmation of this comes from the Annals of Nebopolassar. He described the campaign and concluded with a description of the looting of the city. "The spoil of the city, a quantity beyond counting, they plundered, and turned the city into a mound and a ruin."[6]

After depicting the national disaster, Nahum describes the plight of individuals (Nahum 2:10-13). He gives first a general description (2:10), followed by derision (2:11-12), and culminates in the Lord's declaration (2:13).

As judgment falls, the hearts of the people fail them for fear. Their consciences rise up to condemn them. It seems as if someone has twisted their stomachs into corkscrews. Their knees knock together. The blood drains from their faces. The specter of their past atrocities rises up to confront them.[7] It is a case of the bully finding himself forced into a fight with someone bigger and stronger than himself. Although in the past no one had dared to oppose the might of Assyria (and Nahum, in derision, uses the figure of a

---

6. See *Ancient Near Eastern Texts*, pp. 303-05. A tablet called the Gadd Chronicle in the British Museum further describes the debacle. The armies "launched a powerful attack on the city and in the month Abu the city was taken.. They made great [slaughter] of the prince.... They took a heavy weight of booty from the city and the temple [and turned] the city into a mound and a ruin...." For the full text, see D. J. Wiseman, *Chronicles of the Chaldean Kings* (London: British Museum, 1961), pp. 13-18.

"lion" making forays without fear of its den being molested), now, the people can expect no mercy.

It is to such that the Lord utters His declaration (2:13). He is against them, therefore, they cannot prosper. The things which they have relied on will not help them now. No longer will they be permitted to prey on the weaker nations; and messengers such as Rabshakeh will never again demand their submission (2 Kings 18:17,19; 19:9, 23).

The Dark Side of Life

This description of Nineveh's devastation has led some to question the character of God. How can He be so cruel and heartless? Then, feeling embarrassed at their own audacity, they try to vindicate God by blaming Nahum. After all, he is the one who wrote the book and rejoiced at Assyria's misfortunes.

In responding to this charge, we must not overlook or ignore God's justice. His character requires that He punish those who have violated His laws. In the case of Nineveh, they had manifested an unrepentant attitude. They had sup-

---

7. For a description of the lion-like conquests of Ashurbanipal II, see G. Rawlinson, *The Seven Great Monarchies of the Ancient Eastern World*, I:278-80; and D. D. Luckenbill, *Ancient Records of Assyria and Babylonia*, I:146-48. And for Shalmaneser III and Ashurbanipal, see Luckenbill, *Ancient Records*, I:213 and II:319ff.

pressed the truth and persisted in their sin. Now judgment is to be in kind. Lest anyone be inclined to think of God as capricious, let it be observed that His standards had been established in advance. His moral "law" had been written in their hearts (Romans 1:18-32). Now they must experience the penalty that accompanies waywardness and rejection of His grace. Dr. Gleason L. Archer's observation must also be noted. He pointed out that those who are quick to censure Nahum for his seemingly heartless attitude toward Nineveh demonstrate a basic misunderstanding of the position that God's prophets occupy. "Because [Nahum] is a man of God, he speaks as one who is wholly occupied with the Lord's cause on earth. His earnest desire is to see Jehovah vindicate His holiness in the eyes of the heathen, as over against the inhuman and ruthless tyranny of that God-defying empire which had for so long a time trampled upon all the subject nations with heartless brutality. Only by a crushing and exemplary destruction of Assyria could the world be taught that might does not, in the long run, make right, and that even the mightiest infidel is absolutely helpless before the judicial wrath of Yahweh."[8]

Dr. Archer then continues to describe the remarkable accuracy of Nahum's prophecy. "The fact that the God of Israel could predict with such startling accuracy the fact and the manner of Nineveh's fall was best calculated to prove to

---

8. G. L. Archer, Jr., *A Survey of Old Testament Introduction* (Chicago: Moody, 1974), p. 353.

the ancient world the sovereignty of the one true God. It was a most remarkable reversal of fortune for the proud, pagan capitol to fall to its enemies within less than two decades after the reign of the mighty Ashurbanipal. In just fourteen years after his decease in 626 B.C., the apparently invincible empire which he had so successfully maintained toppled to its ruins, never to rise again."[9]

The Relevance Of It All

But how does all of this apply to us?

In spite of the present economic uncertainty, we in America are living in an era of unparalleled affluence. We enjoy relative social, economic and interpersonal ease. Our wars have invariably been fought on foreign shores. We "have it made," and this very attitude makes us vulnerable. We tend to become insensitive to issues of morality and the abuse of freedom. To the degree that our formative years were in a relatively stable and secure environment, with a strong parent-child love relationship, we are less likely to exploit others or ignore their hurts. But when materialistic values become part of the fiber of life, it is easy for us to gravitate towards self-satisfaction and the acquisition of material possessions. We, therefore, presently occupy a position which bears striking similarities to the social milieu of the ancient Assyrians. And when we take a sober look at

---

9. Ibid.

the environment in which our sons and daughters are being reared, the picture becomes alarming. The work ethic of a generation or two ago has been discarded. Christian influence has declined. False faiths are everywhere apparent. The emphasis is on the temporal to the exclusion of the eternal.

What then is God's attitude toward our open violation of His law, our flagrant disregard for His Word, the perversion of justice, and the exploitation of others?

Because God is unchanging, the conclusion has to be the same as His attitude toward Nineveh. One does not have to be a Christian to recognize the reality of this truth. In an after dinner speech, one social scientist said, "Fundamentally, the force that rules the world is conduct, whether it be moral or immoral. If it is moral, at least there may be hope for the world. If immoral, there is not only no hope, but no prospect of anything but destruction of all that has been accomplished during the last 5,000 years."

But "morality" is derived from principles or absolutes, and these have been communicated to us by God Himself. They have been incorporated in His Word for all to read. All moral obligation resolves itself into the obligation of conformity to the will of God and finds expression in William Penn's dictum that "right is right, even if everyone is against it; and wrong is wrong, even if everyone is for it."

With the example of Nineveh staring us in the face, and realizing our own proneness to commit similar errors, how then may we rear our children? In what way may we develop in them the values they will need to possess?

The key to proper child-rearing is to follow these God-given principles ourselves and instill in our children from birth the ideals of reverence for God and His Word, personal honesty and integrity, loyalty to their country, the importance and dignity of work, love for one another, faithful stewardship of the things the Lord has entrusted to them, and zeal for His cause.

INTERACTION

1. There are times in our lives--particularly times of difficulty, doubt, and uncertainty--when it is hard for us to believe that "all things God works for the good of those who love Him" (Romans 8:28). How may those in Judah have felt during their long years of oppression? Why had God allowed them to be oppressed? In what ways did He now encourage them? How may God's promise of fruitfulness and blessing be enjoyed by us?

2. As our sons and daughters reach adolescence, they come to realize that maturity involves making choices. Discuss some of the choices and decisions your children, regardless of their age or level of development, are even now being faced with. What may they yet have to face? What light does the experience of those in both Assyria

and Judah shed on this issue? How did God deal with them? What may we, as parents, learn from His approach?

3. People of all ages and in all walks of life prefer to rely on themselves or other things rather than on the Lord. Assyria, for example, relied on her defenses. What is the fallacy of such a trust? What happens to us mentally, emotionally and volitionally when we are "let down" by either the people in whom or the things in which we have trusted? How may this be remedied in our lives? Share some of your ideas on how we may develop in our children a genuine trust in and reliance upon the Lord.

4. Mankind has invariably abused the freedom given him by God. "Freedom" tends to be equated with "doing as we please" (cf. Galatians 5:13). In John 8:32 the Lord Jesus--the only free Man who ever lived--said, "If you hold to My teaching, you are really My disciples. Then you will know the truth, and the truth will make you free." Discipleship is like the helmsman of a sailboat exercising his freedom in relation to determining the power of the wind, and navigating his craft so that he reaches his desired destination. Assyria misused her privileges and God held her accountable for her sins. What are some of Christ's truths we as parents may teach our children to help them "navigate" the troublesome currents of life and, through the correct use of

freedom, overcome the temptations and challenges which they will face?

5. Example or "modeling" is the finest form of instruction. In the early years of a child's development, a Christian parent influences his son or daughter more by what he is than by what he teaches. Later on, as a child grows, he needs to know the reason for certain actions. Even at this age, a godly example is vitally important. Discuss some ways in which your parents set you an example. How have you built upon the foundation they laid in the rearing of your own children?

NOTES

Chapter 12

CRABGRASS ON THE LAWN OF LIFE

"Children," we are told, "are the heritage of the Lord" (Psalm 127:3). Today, however, many young couples are opting for childless marriages. Various reasons are given, many of them in place of the real one. In order to assess the attitude of parents toward children, a national survey was taken. The response was staggering. Most of those who returned the questionnaire evidenced bitterness and disappointment. Seventy percent stated that if they had the opportunity to do it all over again, they would not have children. The most candid comments came from older couples. They felt that their children were selfish, thankless and disrespectful. Some even claimed that their children had ruined their marriage.

The problem confronting us is not new. Many social workers and welfare agencies place the blame for a child's improper development squarely on the parents. They echo the words of John Locke who stated, "Parents wonder why the streams are bitter when they themselves have poisoned the fountain." To be sure, one's heredity and environment play an important part in the development of the child, but does this eliminate responsibility on the part of the individual?

One young woman was advised to see a psychoanalyst. From her tests he found that she was markedly hostile and, as her therapy progressed, she became increasingly aware of the bitterness she cherished towards her parents. In the course of her therapy, her analyst tried to get her to express her animosity toward her parents by blaming them for the way she felt and the problems she faced. This was something the young woman found hard to accept. Finally, in desperation, she turned to her analyst and said, "But surely I am responsible for my actions and the way I feel." She went on to point out that if she continued to blame her parents for everything, she would be perpetuating her dependence on them. She realized correctly that part of growing towards maturity entailed accepting responsibility for her actions.

This principle of personal responsibility falls on everyone. The challenge to us as Christian parents is to provide an environment conducive to growth, and to lead our sons and daughters to account properly for their actions. Even the child whose home life has been unhappy can begin to grow as a person as he or she accepts responsibility for his or her own actions.

Blunt Words

In reading through Nahum chapter 3 we notice first that the prophet's passionate description of the destruction of Nineveh (ch. 2) now gives way to a reasoned explanation for her fall. As the "mistress of the nations," she has been guilty of cruelties that have caused her to be feared for her bloodthirstiness. She has become known for her deception and rapine. Nations have been deluded into making treaties and alliances with her, only to find that these pacts have not been kept (2 Kings 18:31; 2 Chronicles 28:21). Those on whom she has "preyed" have been rendered completely helpless by her lies. She has engaged in murder and oppression, the wresting of authority from subject powers and wars out of covetousness. Now she is to be held accountable for her sins.

When we apply the principle of *accountability* to the problem of rearing our children, we begin to realize that behavior must be anchored in God's standards, not in expediency or getting ahead. This basic orientation is vital to proper development. Obedience, however, should not be the result of compulsion. If it is, our children, on reaching adolescence, will experience a natural desire to rebel against imposed standards. Their "waywardness" will be a direct result of the fact that they have never internalized the principles we have attempted to instill in them. The key to personal and moral growth, therefore, lies in parents who will accept God's standards themselves and then encourage and give their children opportunities to make these standards their own through graduated experiences in decision making.

Assyria never accepted God's laws. As a nation, she stockpiled her resources and became wealthy through the exploitation of others. When Nahum uttered his prediction, she turned a deaf ear. She had long since stifled the voice of conscience. A judicial hardening had settled on her people, and all that remained was the punishment their malicious practices so justly deserved.

No Compromise

As judgment falls on the guilty city, no quarter is given. The scene is a graphic one. "The crack of the whip, the rumble of wheels, galloping horses and bounding chariots! Horsemen charging, swords flashing, spears gleaming, many [Ninevites] slain and a mass of dead bodies–there is no end to their number–so much so that they stumble over their corpses."

With this vivid account of what is to happen, Nahum further vindicates God's actions. He likens Nineveh to a society prostitute (Nahum 3:4) and indicts her for her immoral liaisons. He portrays her as decked out in her finery and using her charms to seduce and entice the nations before completely ruining them. As the late Dr. Walter Maier pointed out, "The city's magnificence, the splendor of its palaces and temples, its mighty armies, fabulous wealth, imposing art and architecture--all these are attractions which the brazen adulteress employs in luring victims to their destruction."[1]

---

1. W. Maier, *The Book of the Prophet Nahum* (St. Louis: Concordia, 1959), p. 302.

The biblical image of a prostitute is most uncomplimentary. She is described as an adventuress who allows herself to be seen in provocative attire (Proverbs 7:10), sits at the intersection of streets (Ezekiel 16: 24-25) or on the doorstep of her own house, and calls out to passersby (Proverbs 9:14-15). She is spoken of as brazen and arrogant, as engaging in riotous and rebellious behavior, and as being of smooth speech and seductive charms (Jeremiah 3:3; Proverbs 2:16; 5:3; 6:24-25; 7:5,11). In the book of Revelation (17:5, 15-17) these descriptive elements are applied politically to the city of "Babylon" which is to deceive, ensnare and debauch the whole world. And what "Babylon" is to be, Nineveh was--a faithless "lover," who betrayed those countries that trusted in her.

God speaks against the political alliances which Assyria made with other nations (Isaiah 33:1-3; Hosea 7:7). She promised favors for a price and led her "paramours" to believe that she could be persuaded to oppress other nations on their behalf. Through her lies, she affected the destiny of many peoples. God shows that He is not unmindful of her deeds and now enters into judgment of her for her sins.

From Nahum's poetic description we can easily imagine God as "Judge," sitting on His bench reviewing Nineveh's crimes before passing sentence.

Because of the countless [acts of] fornication of the prostitute---graceful and of deadly charms--who betrays nations through her immoral practices and families through her sorceries ... I will lift up your skirts over your face, and show to the nations your nakedness, and to the kingdoms your disgrace. And I will throw abominable filth on you and make you a spectacle. And it will come to pass that all who see you will shrink from you and say, "Nineveh is devastated! Who will grieve for her?"

The sentence is an appropriate one. From a text such as Hosea 2:3,9-10 (and others like Isaiah 47:2-3 and Ezekiel 16:37-38; 23:29 where reference is obviously to a social custom) it seems as if in times of moral reform, a harlot was stripped of her clothes and expelled from her home or city.[2] Tacit confirmation of this comes from a clay tablet found at Nuzi (a city of Old Testament times whose culture sheds considerable light on Bible customs). This tablet recounts a family squabble and ends with the husband stating that if his wife has an affair with another man,[3] his sons are to strip off her clothes and drive her from the house.

When this truth is applied to Nineveh, we find that retribution is to be in kind. As she subjected other nations to shame and embarrassment, so she is to be treated in the eyes of the world (Nahum 3:5b-6). But this is not all. In the same way that the Assyrians frequently paraded their captives

---

2. See D. R. Hillers, "Treaty-Curses and the Old Testament," *Biblica et Orientalia* (1964), pp. 58f.
3. C. H. Gordon, "Nuzi Tablets Relating to Women," *Miscellanea Orientalia Dedicata Antonio Deimel* (Rome: Pontifical Biblical Institute, 1935).

through the city--sometimes completely naked to add to their humiliation--for the amusement of those lining the streets, so they are to be treated. Stones and filth are to be pelted at them, for in God's sight they have become vile (cf. Malachi 2:3). Furthermore, in the same way that their prominent prisoners of war had been placed in cages to be insulted as the gazing stock of the common folk, so they are to be exposed to the scorn and ridicule of the nations.

And yet in all of this there is a touch of pathos. Punishment could have been avoided. The people could have repented of their sins and turned to the Lord. As it is, they brought judgment on themselves. With a note of compassionate regret, God says, "Where will I seek comforters for you?" It is as if He exclaims with a sigh, "You brought this on yourselves."

Retrospect and Prospect

God's indictment of Nineveh serves to illustrate the exceeding sinfulness of sin. He was anxious to pardon them. They, however, disregarded his warning and rejected His grace. In doing so, they demonstrated their rebelliousness. They wished to be left alone to do as they pleased. They felt confident that they could maintain their independence indefinitely. They, therefore, continued to act in complete disregard of the rights of others--God's as well as man's. And this is where the "cult of self" and its accompanying irresponsibility may be seen most clearly.

The fact that Nahum made this prediction more than two and a half millennia ago does not mean that what God said through him has no application to us today. Nor should we conclude that "we are different" and would never do such things. Human nature is still the same. What we do affects others. That is why Marian Evans (writing under the pseudonym of George Eliot) stated so emphatically, "There is no sort of wrong deed of which a man can bear the punishment alone; you cannot isolate yourself and say that the evil which is in you shall not spread. Men's lives are as thoroughly blended with each other as the air they breathe; evil spreads as a disease."[4] As the Apostle Paul pointed out, "No one lives to himself, and no one dies to himself" (Romans 14:7). Actions have consequences. Whatever we do affects the lives of others.

Accountability, therefore, is inevitable. This principle is illustrated for us by Dr. C. W. Brown in his book, *The Cap and the Gown.* Dr. Brown points out, "Never by any ill chance will two and two make only three and a half; never by any amount of coaxing or stretching four and a half, but always has been so and always will be. There is no shuffling or chance in the moral world. Impulses lead to choice; choices become habits; habits harden speedily into character; and character determines destiny!"[5]

---

4. G. Eliot, *Adam Bede* (New York: Harper, 1885).
5. Source unknown.

Even as the laws which govern the moral world are changeless, so God's absolutes are changeless. And when He moved the apostle Paul to write, "he who sows to the flesh will of the flesh reap corruption" (Galatians 6:8), He meant exactly what He said.

On a recent trip to Geneva, Switzerland, one of the writers passed by the stately mansion once occupied by Lord Byron. After his marriage ended in legal separation (due to Byron's incestuous relationship with his sister), he left England in disgrace, never to return. While in Switzerland, he wrote to a friend. After describing the ideal weather, he went on to say,

> I was disposed to be pleased. I am a lover of nature and an admirer of beauty. I can bear fatigue and welcome privation, and have seen some of the noblest views in the world. But in all this the recollection of bitterness, and more especially of recent and more home desolation which must accompany me through life, has preyed on me here; and neither the music of the shepherd, the crashing of the avalanche, nor the torrent, the mountain, the glacier, the forest, nor the cloud, have for one moment lightened the weight on my heart, nor enabled me to lose my own wretched identity in the majesty, and the

power, and the glory, around, above, and beneath me.[6]

A few years later, at the age of 36, as Byron lay dying, he wrote remorsefully,

> My life is in the yellow leaf,
> The fruits and flowers of life are gone;
> The worm, the canker, and the grief
> Are mine alone.[7]

And as we apply the teaching of Nahum to such a situation, there comes the word of the Lord, "Where shall I seek those who will mourn your passing? You brought this on yourself. It did not have to happen this way."

If we are to avoid similar tragedy, we, as individuals will need

> ... a principle within,
> Of watchful, godly fear,
> A sensibility of sin,
> A pain to feel it near.[8]

---

6. H. H. Brougham, *Recollections of a Long Life* ... (Published privately by the author in 1865).
7. *The Works of Lord Byron* ... (London: Murray, 1832-33).
8. Hymn by Charles Wesley, "I Want a Principle Within" (1749).

We also need to say with Charles Wesley . . .

> Help me the first approach to feel
> Of pride or wrong desire;
> To catch the wandering of my will,
> And quench the kindling fire.[9]

The Wise and the Foolish

When these truths are applied to the task of leading our children to maturity, we need to remember that personal integrity--God's principles internalized and reproduced--cannot be understood in terms of the world's system of values. Integrity has the essence of eternity about it, and only with the passing of time can its true worth be known. Integrity comes from within, and yet it is seen by what we do--the right choices, honest living, trustworthy friendships, and respect for self and others, so that we may enjoy healthy interpersonal relationships.

The question, however, remains: In what specific ways may we, as parents, guide our sons and daughters towards mature adulthood? How may we take these principles from the third chapter of Nahum and translate them into practical guidelines for our interpersonal relationships in the home?

---

9. Ibid.

The answer to these questions may be said to be two-fold and involve both *commitment* and *conduct*. A commitment to what is right is foundational. In Christian homes, where the Word of God is taught, a commitment on the part of a child can occur as early as ages three or four. However, regardless of the age at which the commitment is made, it can result in appropriate conduct as it provides the child's basic orientation to life. Such a life is characterized by integrity. Integrity stands in the way of moral decay. It involves "living by the Book," keeping one's word, being dependable even under pressure and, instead of seeking selfish goals and temporal rewards, looking to the future and a coming day of reward (Hebrews 11:26).

Because integrity is vitally related to the bearing of responsibility, we, as Christian parents, should provide opportunities for our children to make decisions appropriate to their age levels. We can help prepare them for these opportunities in discussions of actual issues and the values upon which their decisions are made.

These times of discussion can focus on attitudes and relationships at home or in the church, at school or while they are with their friends, as well as their sporting activities or hobbies. They should also lead them to evaluate what they see or hear according to their own developing standards so they will not easily be persuaded in their thinking solely by what others say.

In developing this kind of sensitivity to different situations, the family circle can become an open arena for the discussion of moral, behavioral and spiritual issues. It can become a "forum" which will also provide us with an opportunity to interact with them about boy-girl relationships, the connection between principles and practice, the sacredness of their service of the Lord, and the ways in which they can assume increasing responsibility.

During these family discussions, our children should feel sufficiently secure in their relationship with us to disagree with us. When this happens, our response is crucial, for it tacitly demonstrates how secure we feel (a) in our role as parents, (b) in our system of values, and (c) in our ability to reason with our children. In all situations, we should bear in mind that we lead best when we lead by example. We should avoid being defensive, should encourage our children to share their viewpoints as well as consider ours and be willing to share honestly our uncertainties in areas we have not yet resolved.

But growth toward maturity also involves the bearing of responsibility. In this connection, we should remember that there are different kinds of responsibilities that we can give our children at different stages in their development. As far as possible we should make the carrying out of these responsibilities as fulfilling and meaningful as possible. The varying obligations or tasks we assign to them should provide positive growth experiences for them. These life-situation responsibilities should have a cumulative effect and should be geared towards helping them develop into competent adults. When this happens, they will be able to avoid the errors into which the Assyrians fell and be spared the consequences that overtook those in Nineveh.

This is what growth toward maturity is all about. The immature are always full of excuses. They are perpetually tardy, lacking in convictions and ready to give up the moment the going gets rough. Their lives are strewn with broken promises, unfinished tasks and blighted relationships. Maturity, however, is seen in knowing right from wrong, making right choices, preserving one's principles and living in peace with situations that cannot be changed.

INTERACTION

1. According to the apostle Paul, those living in the last days will be "lovers of themselves, lovers of money, boastful, proud, abusive, disobedient to parents, ungrateful, unholy, without natural affection, unforgiving ..." and the list goes on and on (2 Timothy 3:2-5). What opposing virtues do we desire to instill in our children? (See 2 Timothy 2:22-26). How can we bring our children to understand the negative consequences of Paul's list of vices without simply preaching at them?

2. Some modern writers tell us that "morality" (i.e., ethical standards) is relative. "There is no such thing as right

and wrong. And this makes morality a personal and cultural phenomenon." How would those living in Nineveh at the time of Nahum have reacted to such a statement? What is the testimony of history? Where may we find principles to guide our conduct and destiny that are free from cultural bias? What is the best way to begin implementing these principles?

3. As noted in the previous chapter, we should encourage our children in the development of responsible autonomy. This expanding awareness of their abilities should be based upon a full and free commitment of themselves to God's design for their lives. Such progress can be greatly encouraged by giving them opportunities to make decisions that affect their lives and that are appropriate to their level of ability and understanding.

4. Describe some of the ways we can give our children these kinds of opportunities (described in 3 above) at the primary, intermediate, and adolescent levels of growth. What knowledge will they require if they are to make these decisions wisely? What values would you desire them to have to guide their decision making? What is your basis (biblical versus cultural) for these values?

5. The Word of God encourages those who are new converts to Christianity (i.e., "babes in Christ") to "crave the pure milk [of the Word] so that by it they might

grow" (1 Peter 2:2). As we develop, however, our "diet" changes. We need "solid food" (1 Corinthians 3:1-3; Hebrews 5:13-14). How do we apply this truth to the Bible training we give our children? Choose an age group and structure your own "curriculum" for a year. Define its aim, select appropriate Scripture passages to build upon, and brainstorm on ways you might carry it out.

NOTES

Chapter 13

MATURITY, INTERDEPENDENCE AND HOPE

A pastor was called by a hospital to visit an attempted suicide--a young woman--who was a member of his church. He hurried to the hospital and quickly obtained the facts from the doctor. They included a heavy dose of aspirin, probably half a bottle, and a slashed wrist.

Sitting by Susan's bedside, he allowed her to tell her own story. "My life has been a sham," she confessed. "I am a better-than-average student in college. I've been involved with Inter Varsity, and all that. I enjoy my studies; and you know that I'm involved in just about everything at the church. But it has all been an act--a convincing one that has kidded everyone, even me. I don't believe in God, at least not until now. I find it hard to believe that He loves me; He's so distant and unseen. And I have nothing to convince me that I can know Him. Well, to try and fill life with something meaningful and satisfying, I turned first to drinking and then to sex. At times I would feel guilty, but I would suppress these feelings or else I'd explain them away as just 'old fashioned' or as part of a 'parent' conscience telling me, as my parents had done so often, that the things I was doing were wrong.

"A few months ago my life began to come apart at the seams. I began feeling depressed. I became ill. I did not know what was wrong. Then my boyfriend broke up with me because I was no longer fun to be with. With no one to turn to, I determined to end it all. I took the aspirin to deaden any pain. But when I saw the blood on my wrist, I became sick to my stomach and ran for help. Oh, pastor, how I wish there was someone who cared for me and loved me. I've ruined my life! I feel lonely and afraid."

How tragic. So young and yet finding out the hard way that what God has said in His Word about the way of a transgressor being hard (Proverbs 13:15) is true. Susan's basic problem, as reflected in her initial comments to her pastor, show her refusal to believe the Lord and look to Him as her Source of purpose and direction in life. Though she appeared to be a believer to others, she had never acknowledged the sovereignty of God in her heart. Lacking spiritual life within, she vainly tried to find meaning and fulfillment through her own efforts: playing at being a Christian to win the approval of her parents and friends, and then privately turning to self-satisfying experiences in a vain attempt to fill the emptiness within.

But Susan's story has a happy ending. Lying on her hospital bed she poured out her heart to a God she was not sure was there. She begged Him to help her. She asked Him for faith to believe. Finally she trusted herself to Him. And in her own words she said, "I was surprised when peace filled me. I no longer felt tortured in my mind; my anxieties were gone; it was as if a warm blanket of love had been wrapped around me."

In her experience Susan proved the truth of God's words that those who "come to Him, He will certainly not cast out" (John 6:37). God's forgiveness became so meaningful to her that in time she was able to forgive herself. She later married, and is now a devoted Christian wife and mother.

What of Nineveh

Susan found that God was gracious and compassionate, slow to anger and abundant in lovingkindness (Jonah 4:2). She turned to Him in the hour of her need and experienced the pardon the Assyrians refused.

As we consider God's indictment of Nineveh in the closing section of Nahum's prophecy (3:8-19), two themes run together. The one is the certainty that God's Word will be fulfilled, and the other is that all earthly hope is vain. Nahum's message came to the people of Assyria at the height of Ashurbanipal's reign. He had established his nation's supremacy so that no nation dared lift so much as a finger against them. Nahum's prophecy, however, was one of pending judgment, and he imagines those in Nineveh asking scornfully, "Who is this God who can do these things to us?"

The question, of course, has been answered already (1:14; 2:1-2), but it is fully in keeping with human nature to pay scant attention to things we do not want to hear. God, therefore, graciously repeats Himself. But this time there is no final word of regret (cf. 3:7). Instead of pointing to nature and giving demonstration after demonstration of His power and might (1:2-8), He turns the searchlight on Assyria and asks, "Are you more securely located than No-Amon [i.e., Thebes] who was ensconced among the rivers with water surrounding her, whose rampart was the sea [i.e., the broad expanse of an inland lake] and the sea [i.e., the Nile] her wall?" In other words, God asks, "Are your defenses superior? Are you more strategically situated? Is Asher greater than Amon [god of the sun] that he can protect you?"

No-Amon, or Thebes as she is better known, was dedicated to the worship of the sun god, Amon-Re, and reference to her as "No-Amon" (or in Egyptian, Ne-Amon) merely means "the city of Amon." No-Amon was one of the renowned cities of antiquity. The ruins of Luxor and Karnak today mark the site of this ancient metropolis. Homer, in his *Iliad*, refers to her as having one hundred gates;[1] and the great Egyptologist, Sir Flinders Petrie, wrote glowingly of her temples.[2]

---

1. Homer, *The Iliad*, IX:381-84. Homer's "one hundred gates" is undoubtedly a reference to the many entrances leading into the temples of Karnak and Luxor.

Thebes (or No-Amon) straddled the Nile. The royal necropolis occupied the western bank of the Nile, while the city proper developed around the temples on the eastern bank. Thebes enjoyed excellent defenses. The river Nile branched out into four channels, and an artificial lake (called by Nahum a "sea" approximately one mile long and 350 yards wide) formed formidable barriers to an invading army. In addition, Thebes had military alliances with the Libyans, Ethiopians, and Somalis (ancient Put). Yet, in spite of these strengths, she was destined to be destroyed. The religious and political corruption practiced within her walls incurred the anger of God. Speaking through Isaiah the prophet, He outlined the downward course of her history and her eventual overthrow by Assyria (Isaiah 19:1-15). These events began to be fulfilled under Esarhaddon. When Esarhaddon died, his son, Ashurbanipal, took command of the Assyrian armies. Listen as he tells the story.

> In my first campaign I marched against Egypt and Ethiopia. Tirhakah, king of Egypt and Nubia, whom Esarhaddon, king of Assyria, my own father, had defeated and in whose country he (Esarhaddon) had ruled, this (same) Tirhakah forgot the might of Ashur, Ishtar and the (other) great gods, my lords, and put his trust upon his own power. He turned against the kings (and) regents

---

2. W. M. F. Petrie, *Six Temples of Thebes* (London: Quaritch, 1897).

> whom my own father had appointed in Egypt. He entered and took residence in Memphis, the city that my own father had conquered and incorporated into Assyrian territory. An express messenger came to Nineveh to report to me. I became very angry on account of these happenings and my soul was aflame. I lifted up my hands, prayed to Ashur and the Assyrian Ishtar. (Then) I called on my mighty armed forces which Ashur and Ishtar had entrusted to me and took the shortest road to Egypt and Nubia.[3]

In his annals, Ashurbanipal describes the defeat of Tirhakah at Memphis and how he followed him to Thebes. "This town (too) I seized and led my army into it to repose (there)." He then appointed rulers in the different cities and required that the people give him the honor of suzerain. This they promised to do, but as soon as his armies withdrew, they rebelled. It was therefore necessary for him to invade Egypt a second time. This time he was more ruthless than before.

> In my second campaign I marched directly against Egypt and Nubia. Urdamane heard of the approach of my expedition (only when) I had (already) set foot on Egyptian territory.

---

3. *Ancient Near Eastern Texts*, p. 294.

He left Memphis and fled into Thebes to save his life. The kings, governors, and regents whom I had installed in Egypt came to me and kissed my feet. I followed Urdamane (and) went as far as Thebes, his fortress. He saw my mighty battle array approaching, left Thebes, and fled to Kipkipi. Upon a trust (-inspiring) oracle of Ashur and Ishtar, I, myself, conquered this town completely. From Thebes I carried away booty, heavy and beyond counting: silver, gold, precious stones, his entire personal possessions, linen garments with multi-colored trimmings, fine horses, (certain) inhabitants, male and female. I pulled two high obelisks, cast of shining *Lahalu-bronze,* the weight of which was 2,500 talents, standing at the door of the temple, out of their bases and took (them) to Assyria. (Thus) I carried off from Thebes heavy booty, beyond counting. I made Egypt and Nubia feel my weapons bitterly and celebrated my triumph. With full hands and safety, I returned to Nineveh, the city (where I exercised) my rule.[4]

---

4. *Ibid.,* p. 295. See also J. H. Breasted, *History of Egypt* (New York: Scribner's, 1937), pp. 550-59.

And so Thebes fell to the Assyrians in accordance with the word of the Lord.

No Place to Hide

How does all of this apply to Nineveh? In the light of the experience of Thebes, does the proud city on the banks of the Tigris River feel that she will escape the judgment that has been determined for her?

In indicting Nineveh, Nahum uses the same terminology employed by Isaiah (Isaiah 19:14, 16). When judgment overtakes the Assyrians, it will appear to all as if the people are intoxicated. But their state of stupefaction will be due to the heavy blows of the Almighty[5] rather than the effect of fermented wine (Nahum 3:12). In this state, the city will fall to the invaders as easily as ripe figs fall from the tree. The people will also seek refuge, a place to hide, but find none.

But what of the city's soldiers--those well-trained men whose presence has instilled fear of a horrible death in all nations from Babylonia to the Mediterranean and Armenia to Egypt? Nahum describes them as "women" (i.e., untrained for war and too weak to handle heavy armor and equipment) who are helpless in the hands of the invaders (3:13). Then, with a touch of irony, he encourages the

---

5. For further information on the "wine of God's wrath," see passages like Revelation 14:10; 16:19; 17:2; 18:3.

inhabitants of Nineveh to prepare for the coming siege, to strengthen the fortifications and to make bricks to close up the breaches that will be made in the wall (3:14).

Ominous Warning

Those in Nineveh, however, ignore the warning. They feel secure. And when Cyaxares attacks them the first time, he is repulsed. This serves to increase their confidence in themselves. It also gives them one more reason to discount the words of the prophet. However, as verse 15*a* indicates, in the place where they imagine themselves to be the most secure, there they will find that their confidence has been misplaced. The destruction which is due to overtake them will be as swift as fire, as final as death (by the sword), and as irresistible as a plague of locusts (cf. Exodus 10:4-19; Joel 2:4-5).[6] Destruction will be complete; nothing will be left.

Having mentioned a swarm of locusts, Nahum then applies the characteristics of a swarm of locusts to (a) the people in the city, 15*b*; (b) the traders, 16; (c) the officials, 17; (d) those who should be looking after the welfare of the people in the city, 18*a*; and (e) those who are fortunate enough to escape, 18*b*.

---

6. See *The National Geographic* (1915), pp. 511-50; *idem*, (1953), pp. 545-62; *idem*, (1969), pp. 202-27.

To the first group Nahum says in effect, "Multiply yourself like the creeping locust; increase your numbers like the swarming locust." If there is to be safety in numbers, then bring into the city everyone you can find, old and young, men and women--in fact, anyone who can aid in the defense of the city.

He then turns to the merchants who, on account of the trade that has passed through Nineveh, have established offices in the capital and become rich as a result. As locusts after emerging from the chrysalis shake off all hindrances and quickly fly away, so these traders will transfer their assets to another city and discard Nineveh as a worn-out cocoon. Their loyalty will be to their balance sheets and not to the city that has made them rich.

The guardsmen of the city exhibit yet another characteristic of the locust--lethargy. Nahum imagines the inactivity of locusts on a cold day. They congregate together waiting for the sun to warm their bodies. As soon as they are warm enough to fly, they are gone. So the watchmen on the walls of the city and the soldiers in the barracks will at first pay no attention to the approaching danger. But when aroused, they will quickly take flight. And what was true of the trained militia will also be true of the king and his nobles. They rest in a false sense of security and are seen in repose when circumstances require that they be planning and organizing the defense of the city.

Finally, those of the people who are able to escape are viewed as having been scattered as locusts when the wind drives them away. Lacking leadership (Proverbs 30:27), they are unable to regroup. And so the city and her people vanish from view. So completely was God's word fulfilled that the early geographer, Strabo, claimed that the city quickly disappeared, and its place was soon forgotten.[7]

God concludes his description of Nineveh's fall with a final pronouncement: "There is no relief for your breakdown, your wound is incurable. All who hear the report about you will clap their hands over you, for on whom has not your evil passed continually?" No one will lament Nineveh's demise. So ruthless have the Assyrians been that when the tyrannical, bloodthirsty city finally meets her nemesis, the nations will actually rejoice over her downfall.

The seriousness of what God has decreed has been applied to nations today by the renowned Bible scholar, Dr. C. F. Keil:

> If Nahum's prophecy was thus fulfilled in the destruction of Nineveh, even to the disappearance of every trace of its existence, we must not restrict it to this one historical event, but must bear in mind that, as the prophet simply saw in Nineveh the represen-

---

7. Strabo, *Geography*, XVI:1:3.

tative for the time of the power of the world in its hostility to God, so the destruction predicted to Nineveh applied to all the kingdoms of the world which have risen up against God since the destruction of Ashur, and which will continue to do so till the end.[8]

And we will do well to remember that the principles that apply to nations apply to individuals as well, for the national character is but the reflection of the desires of the people.

Full Circle

All of this underscores the importance of the two principles mentioned earlier in this chapter; namely, that God's word is sure and will be fulfilled exactly as He said it would, and that human confidences are in vain. Only by identifying ourselves with the Lord and His purpose can we live meaningfully now and have hope for the future. Our task, in leading our children to maturity, is to help them avoid the errors Assyria made.

The fact of God's sovereignty--that what He has predicted He has the power to bring to pass--stirs feelings of rebellion in some people. They feel that this deprives them

---

8. C. F. Keil, *The Twelve Minor Prophets* (Grand Rapids: Eerdmans, n.d.), II:48.

of their freedom of choice. They want to be free to do as they choose. Free will, of course, is what the Assyrians practiced, only to find that actions have consequences. This emphasis on free will is characteristic of the present world system. Christians realize that this type of free expression eventually leads to the kind of inordinate self-indulgence that is contrary to the teaching of the Bible. They, therefore, have tended to avoid all forms of self-expression (resulting in spiritual passivity) and have viewed pleasure as a mark of carnality. Avoidance of all forms of pleasure on the assumption that they were mortifying the flesh led some into a false form of asceticism. But passivity--where God does everything and we do nothing--brings with it its own problems, such as a total lack of spiritual initiative or a critical attitude toward assertive believers. Furthermore, God intended us to be happy and enjoy life; and personal maturity involves choosing the good and rejecting the evil. Unfortunately, the biblical teaching of mature interdependence is rarely heard in most evangelical. circles, and is absent from many homes.

Acknowledging God's sovereignty is vitally connected with mature interdependence. Those who feel that restrictions are evil show by their attitude their immaturity. They read into the limitations placed on them the idea of denial and do not realize that God has a plan and purpose for our enjoyment of the blessings He is waiting to bestow on us. Maturity---mature interdependence--involves: A healthy owning and recognizing of one's strengths.

- An accepting attitude towards one's weaknesses or limitations.

- A willingness to be assertive in a relaxed, spontaneous manner (i.e., assertive, not aggressive, for aggressiveness often shows itself in dominance and a tendency to ride roughshod over others. Assertiveness operates from a position of mutual respect for other people--and living in a relationship of mutual respect with all concerned).

- A readiness to be the strength for someone else as well as being willing to rely upon the strength of another when confronted with or dealing with one's limitations.

- A recognition of the fact that in all of one's behavior the individual is ultimately responsible for his own choices and actions.

A vital faith in (i.e., reliance upon) God and His purpose for us is the best foundation for the development of proper maturity. The world finds that this runs contrary to its value system and often accuses the believer of using his faith as a "crutch"-- believing that in the world you either make it on your own or you "cop out." The former opens the door to all sorts of oppressive and exploitive acts as people claw their way to the top. Assyria serves as a notable example of this.

Believers, on the other hand, may draw on the Lord for their strength and maintain a position of active responsibility as they allow God to work through them to accomplish His purpose. This was the experience of the Psalmist. He said, "God is our refuge and strength, a very present help in trouble" (Psalm 46:1); and David exclaimed, "The LORD is my rock and my fortress and my deliverer, my God, my rock, in whom I take refuge; my shield and the horn of my salvation, my stronghold" (Psalm 18:2). He knew the bitterness of trusting in his own resources (Psalms 22:15; 31:10; 38:10) and came to trust entirely in the Lord as the needs of each day determined (Psalms 18:32, 39; 20:6; 21:1; 22:19-21; 27:1-3; 28:7-8; etc.). All of this was in contrast to the ways of godless men who did not make God their trust (Psalm 52:1-7).

Instead of trust in God being a "crutch" to support a cripple, this kind of relationship--of willing submission to His sovereignty and mature interdependence in dealing with others--helps the believer fulfill his responsibilities and live life up to the limit of his capacities.

Real Possibilities

Our children learn maturity from us. At birth they are helpless and totally dependent. As they grow, they early exhibit a desire to do things for themselves. Wise parents will, therefore, increase the opportunities for their children to cultivate their abilities, develop their strengths and work on their weaknesses. Ideally, this would be in an environment of loving encouragement, understanding, acceptance of failure, and the application of necessary limits appropriate to their ages and development.

As a child moves first into early adolescence (and then into middle and late adolescence), the wise parent will adjust the amount of parental oversight. A greater portion of control and direction will be given the child while the parent adopts more and more a posture of less restraint coupled with wise counsel. In this role the parent is more the adviser and less the controlling influence. Ultimately, the child is released to experience fully his growing autonomy as an emerging adult.

Throughout the process, we see our children developing true interdependence, combining self-reliance with an awareness of their limitations, and, as they commit their lives to Christ, finding in Him the foundation and focus for their growth toward maturity. The result is the development of a godly self-perception, establishment of healthy relationships, the blossoming of a meaningful life and the avoidance of the self-centeredness that paved the way for Nineveh's downfall.

INTERACTION

1. Brainstorm on some of the promises as well as some of the warnings mentioned in the Bible. Write these down. What other Scriptures support these divine pronouncements? How sure are they of fulfillment? In view of these "blessings and cursings" (cf. Deuteronomy 11:26-28; 28:8; 30:1-10, 19), and the examples of both Assyria and Judah, what changes do you feel should be made in your life-style? How do you plan to implement these changes?

2. What are some of the earthly or temporal things in which we are inclined to trust? What are some of the things in which people and/or nations trusted in Bible times (e.g., Ruth 2:12; 2 Samuel 22: 2ff., 31; 2 Kings 18:5, 20-24; Psalm 22:4-5; Isaiah 47:10; Jeremiah 5:17; 49:4*b*; etc.)? What circumstances do these incidents describe? What principles do these illustrate? How does all this apply to us today?

3. In Assyria, as in our own country, certain attitudes ultimately became established patterns of behavior and brought upon the nation the judgment of God. What are some parallels that you have observed in your study of Jonah and Nahum? How can you counteract these tendencies in your own life as well as in the life of your son or daughter?

4. God desires our growth toward maturity (1 Thessalonians 4:3). In what ways is our acceptance of God's sovereignty connected with this process? How does this contribute to the development of mature interdependence?

5. James described a tendency many of us have shown at one time or another--a tendency to be forgetful of the lessons God the Father is trying to teach us (James 1:21*b*-25). What we need is continuous exposure to His Word (note Hebrews 5:12-14 where the use we make of the Scripture is directly related to our maturity). Given your situation at home, what is the best way for you to attend to your personal growth? How is this likely to affect your children?

NOTES

www.ingramcontent.com/pod-product-compliance
Lightning Source LLC
Chambersburg PA
CBHW062016220426
43662CB00010B/1358